Dear Dana

~

FREQUENTLY ASKED QUESTIONS ABOUT DATING AFTER NARCISSISTIC ABUSE

~

How to Avoid the Wrong People, have a Wildly Fulfilling Relationship with the Right One, and Learn to Love Yourself along the Way

DANA MORNINGSTAR

Morningstar Media
PO Box 464 Mason, MI 48854

Printed in the United States of America

First Printing, 2020

Morningstar Media

PO Box 464

Mason, MI 48854

Dedication

To everyone who has experienced abuse, please know that just because someone else couldn't or wouldn't treat you with kindness and care doesn't mean that you aren't worthy of it, it means that they are deeply damaged. Healthy, well-adjusted people don't go around destroying others. You matter and are worthy of being treated with dignity and respect simply because you are alive...and please don't ever listen to anyone who tries to tell you otherwise.

I am not what happened to me, I am what I
choose to become.

~ Carl Jung

Acknowledgements

I have to start by thanking my wonderful editor, sounding board, and valued friend, Marisol. From reading early drafts, being patient with the fits and starts my writing process moves in, to giving advice on the cover, as well as helping to shape the questions and answers in a way that would provide the most benefit to the reader, she was as important to this book getting done as I was. I am so glad to have met you in this lifetime and am even more thrilled that I get the opportunity to work with you. Thank you so much for everything you do.

And, of course, thank you to my dear friend, administrator of the support group, sound engineer, cook, and fiancé, Paul. I can only imagine how challenging being in a relationship with a writer must be. I appreciate your patience, understanding, and support, and it means the world to me that we are able to grow this dream together.

Table of Contents

Preface

Like most non-fiction writers, my book ideas come from a place of deep personal interest in the topic, and a driving desire to share all of the hard-won lessons learned along the way. When I tried to piece together my own life, I became fully aware of just how emotionally lost at sea I was and, as a result, how difficult it can be to heal from psychological and emotional abuse. I spent hundreds of hours feverishly searching for validation, answers, closure, peace, some sense of normalcy, hope…I wasn't even sure. I just knew that I had so many questions, but struggled to put them into words. Thankfully, other survivors were willing to share their experiences, lessons, and advice, which helped me in ways far greater than I had hoped, expected, or even realized I needed.

After getting a solid footing in my own recovery, I started my own support group, which has now grown to over 50,000 members. Over time, I couldn't help but notice that variations of the same questions were asked repeatedly. What was powerful, was that the answers to their questions not only gave them the validation and clarity they were looking for, it was as though they were set free from some invisible trap that survivors so often find themselves.

In an effort to make it easier to grasp the tremendous amount of information that is involved in narcissistic abuse, *Dear Dana: FAQs about Dating After Narcissistic Abuse* is one in a series of books designed for abuse survivors. If you have any questions, comments, concerns, frustrations, ideas for books, or want to share with me your own victories with healing, let me know. I'm always happy to connect with fellow travelers on this path. You can reach me at deardana@thriveafterabuse. com or my website: www.thriveafterabuse.com

Introduction

Before we dive into the questions and answers, I feel it's important to mention that abuse can happen within every dynamic. While the vast majority of the questions I receive come from women who are recovering from abusive relationships with men, anyone can be in an abusive relationship regardless of their gender, sexual orientation, age, religion, nationality, or social-economic status. I mention this not because of political correctness or inclusivity but because it's vital that abuse is seen not only as a women or children's issue, but as a human issue. Until we are able to understand that abuse isn't about gender or strength, but about power and control, then it will continue to remain difficult to identify and even harder to address, assess, and treat.

While identifying abusive behavior (especially narcissistically abusive behavior) for what it is provides its own set of challenges, dating after this type of trauma can be difficult for a variety of reasons, many of which are covered in this book. Even years after the abusive relationship is over, many still feel either numb or repulsed by the idea of dating. Those wanting to date again may find themselves terrified of getting tangled up with another abusive person.

Being unable to trust our judgment is unnerving and anxiety-producing, especially if our opinion differs from that of others. When we doubt our ability to avoid hurtful people and stay safe, we may feel like someone took a magnet to our internal compass; we don't know which direction to head, and so we don't move forward. We stay in one place, waiting for the day our compass works again, and our confidence and desire to try and have relationships come back.

Those who do move forward and start dating often find

themselves in a series of abusive relationships of varying degrees, but they don't know why. They may fear they attract problematic people, or that they are repaying some unknown karmic debt. The reality is that they are missing some vital information.

As a result, they pour their time into researching everything about narcissists or abusive behavior, thinking that doing so will help them to stay safe in the future. The problem with this is that there is a lot to learn about how to stay safe, and learning about narcissists and/or abuse is only part of it because, what tends to happen is that, despite all of their knowledge, the survivor then becomes tangled up with yet another problematic person. When the survivor realizes this, they become so rattled and discouraged that they avoid meeting new people altogether. This fear and anxiety brings them right back to square one, reading and learning more about narcissists and abusive behavior. The problem with this thinking is that every narcissist or abusive person is different; studying them more isn't what's needed to keep yourself safe.

The good news is that the information that will set you free doesn't have to take years to learn, and these lessons don't have to be learned the hard way, or even learned all at once for your life to begin moving in a positive direction. Perhaps the best place to start the discussion of dating after abuse is to talk about what healing does and doesn't mean in terms of being ready to date again.

What healing after abuse doesn't mean:

1. Healing doesn't mean being completely over your ex.
2. Healing doesn't mean finding other people attractive.
3. Healing doesn't mean having a desire to date or be sexual.

4. Healing doesn't mean you are familiar with some (or even all) of the red flags of abusive behavior.

While these four points are a big step towards healing, being *ready to date again means:*

- Knowing what you are looking for in a partner and not dating because you are lonely, need a friend, or are looking for someone to help you heal.

- Recognizing when you are uncomfortable, knowing when you are being mistreated, used or abused, and how to handle that if it happens.

- Using discernment, and looking for someone who has the more in-depth criteria you are looking for in a life partner (such as shared values, and life direction)—not developing a relationship because, for example, the person is good looking, funny, or even that you share common interests.

- Being able to validate yourself. If you think something is a problem, you don't need others to agree with you, and you are comfortable asserting yourself.

- Knowing the difference between functional and dysfunctional behavior in others, but also within yourself.

- Understanding, having and implementing healthy standards, boundaries, and deal-breakers.

- Not placing your self-esteem in the hands of others. Knowing your value, regardless of whether or not others see it. Separating your self-worth from your hurt feelings so that, if the next relationship ends, you don't feel unlovable, worthless, or suicidal.

- Realizing that a healthy relationship is founded just as much (if not more so) on character, negotiation, team work, assertiveness, appropriate expectations, boundaries, and communication it is on as compatibility.

- Being able to identify and walk away from destructive relationships regardless of how much you care about the other person--understanding that how they treat you is more important than how you feel about them.

- Having a support system, friends, and hobbies outside of this person, so you don't make them your whole world, and knowing it's unhealthy to give up any of these things in order to maintain the relationship.

- Understanding that the foundation of a loving relationship is behavior, particularly respectful, considerate, and appreciative actions. Hurtful behavior (lying, cheating, stealing, etc.) do not belong in a loving relationship, even if half-hearted or grand apologies follow that behavior.

- Understanding that all healthy relationships, at times, have conflict and confrontation, but are handled maturely. The absence of conflict and confrontation is not a sign of a healthy relationship; it's a sign of poor communication.

- Realizing that all relationships are easy to get into and much harder to get out of. For this reason, going slow and using sound judgment are self-protective; moving full speed ahead is not.

If, after reading this list, you feel uncertain about any of these points, don't fret! This book addresses all of the concepts in both detail and context. My goal is that, by the end of this book, you will feel safer and secure when it comes to interacting with others, and you will be well on your way to cultivating the skills necessary to have a fulfilling relationship.

Chapter 1: What are boundaries and how can I tell if mine need work?

Dear Dana,

I thought I had good boundaries, but now I'm questioning if my boundaries need work and I just never realized it before. I'm also thinking that maybe my understanding of what boundaries are isn't as comprehensive as it needs to be. Could you explain what boundaries are and how can I tell if mine need work?

~ Toni

Dear Toni,

Oh, you aren't alone when it comes to being confused about boundaries! And since boundaries a fundamental to healthy relationships, I'm so glad you asked. Most people tend to think of setting boundaries as saying "no." In part this is correct, but it doesn't capture the full concept. Boundaries aren't just verbal, they are also physical, sexual, emotional, psychological, spiritual, and financial. A person's boundaries are both internal and external. I like to think of boundaries as the bodyguards to our standards, as our boundaries dictate what we let in and what we put out into the world.

Instead of referring to boundaries as healthy or unhealthy, I think it's helpful to view them as functional and non-functional. We can tell how functional our boundaries are based on how well our lives are functioning on a daily basis. If our boundaries are functional, then we have an appropriate understanding of what we can and cannot control, as well as where we stop and where others begin. Because of this, our relationships with other people are relatively smooth and we have a good degree of peace in our lives. If our boundaries are not functioning as well as they could be, we struggle with what we are, and are not, responsible or accountable for. As a result, we may feel overly responsible for others, or as though others should be responsible for taking care of us. We may feel like our life is out of our control and that bad events (usually people mistreating or taking advantage of us) continually happen, but we don't know why. This is a stressful way to live, and leads to all kinds of emotional and physical problems, ranging from perpetual confusion, irritation, anger, frustration, rage, anxiety, depression, chronic pain, fatigue, headaches, and so on.

In order to have functional boundaries, we must first have functional standards for our behavior and the behavior of those in our life. And before we can have functional standards, we must have healthy self-esteem. The good news is that we can start making positive adjustments anywhere along this line and those changes will positively impact the other areas. Let's take a step back and examine what functional and non-functional self-esteem, standards, and boundaries look like in motion.

At the core, functional self-esteem means that we believe we are worthy of being treated with dignity and respect—by all people, including ourselves. Once we realize and believe we have value, then our standards will match this, and our boundaries will be the actions we take to ensure we protect ourselves. Some of the ways we protect ourselves are by determining what works for us and what doesn't work for us; what we need and what we don't need; what we allow in and what we keep out. If a person says something hurtful, we might have our feelings hurt, but we don't let it negatively impact our worth as a person. We may feel like lashing out at them, but our boundaries and standards give us the needed self-restraint so that we are able to behave in a way that is in alignment with the type of person we believe ourselves to be. As James Clear, author of the book *Atomic Habits* says, "Every action you take is a vote for the kind of person you want to become." In short, *we have to first understand that we have worth in order for us to protect it.*

So what does valuing ourselves in terms of functional boundaries look like in motion? It might be easiest to understand this concept by thinking about the other people, or things, in your life that you value, such as a dear friend, a valued hobby, or some item of deep personal significance. When we value something, we cherish it. We do our best to keep it safe and secure, and we take care of it. When we value ourselves, we do the same; we are intentional and respectful with our time, body, energy, emotions, thoughts, and actions.

When one of our boundaries is crossed, we experience emotional discomfort. Usually, the degree of discomfort is in proportion to the degree of the boundary violation. (When the degree of discomfort is out of proportion to the boundary violation, this may be a "trigger," or sign of unprocessed emotions or unhealed trauma from a past boundary violation.) Everyone's boundaries are different, which is why we must be able to let someone know if they've crossed a line with us. Some boundaries are more universal than others, for example, most of us understand that it's not okay to flirt with others when we are in a relationship, grab a stranger's crotch, cuss at our boss, customers, or co-workers when we get upset, read a friend's journal, or expect other adults to take care of us financially. Other boundaries vary from person-to-person, such as, one's view of dark humor, how they discipline their children or talk to them about sex, thoughts about loaning money, religion, marriage, and use of strong language, to name a few.

When a person has non-functional or damaged self-esteem, they let in and/or put out a variety of hurtful behavior. They may feel chronic guilt when setting boundaries with others, or have difficulty acknowledging when they are being treated disrespectfully or in a way that isn't okay with them. They don't often assert themselves, and instead either become passive, passive-aggressive, or aggressive. They have trouble telling where responsibility and accountability for themselves and others starts and ends. When boundaries are blurred, then we are most likely tolerating being mistreated by others because we think standing up for ourselves is wrong and means we are selfish or uncompromising. Additionally, when our boundaries are blurred, we may feel responsible for the well-being of others and feel obligated to solve their problems. Either way, having blurred boundaries like this can be emotionally, physically, and financially exhausting. It takes time and practice to become comfortable with boundary-setting, but the result will be a happier life, and stronger personal relationships.

Chapter 2: What is a healthy relationship?

Dear Dana,

I left my ex close to three years ago because he was abusive in every way imaginable. I knew I didn't want to ever be in a relationship like that again, so I went to therapy. During my time there, the therapist helped me clarify some traits I was looking for in a partner. Some of the qualities we came up with were kind, good to kids and animals, attentive, affectionate, considerate, and so on. That was helpful, and I've been dating on and off for about the past eighteen months, but I'm not sure if I know what a healthy relationship is. Outside of looking for a good man, what makes a relationship healthy?

~ Patricia

Dear Patricia,

You bring up a great point that I don't think is made often enough—finding a "good" partner is only one aspect of what makes for a healthy relationship. A healthy relationship is something that grows moment-by-moment between two people. Additionally, it's essential to separate a "good man" (or woman) from a "healthy relationship" because a person can appear good in all the ways that you list, but at the same time be abusive in a relationship or toward others. (At an extreme level, Bill Cosby, Ted Bundy, and the BTK killer all come to mind.)

It is easy to confuse niceness or likability with goodness. It's even more challenging to see how a seemingly good person could be problematic, especially if the person is merely wearing the "good person" mask. The point I'm trying to make is that if you are in a relationship with someone, getting to know their character is important. However, it's just as important to be aware of problems, and know how to handle them as they surface in the relationship.

Before I get into the elements of a healthy relationship, I feel it's important to acknowledge that the term "healthy relationship" is often misunderstood. This leads people to feel defensive or to dismiss the concept altogether, thinking that a "healthy relationship" is an idealized concept that doesn't exist in real life. *If this is you, try instead substituting the words "nourishing" or "functional" for "healthy" to see the concept more clearly.*

A healthy relationship is similar to a healthy plant. We can tell when a plant is healthy because it has a good root base, it's growing, periodically has new blooms, and is thriving where it is. An unhealthy plant has any number of issues going on that are preventing it from growing. There might be moldy soil, the pot is too big or too small, the roots are rotting, the leaves are turning yellow or developing spots, or the plant is wilting due to too much or too little sun or water.

A plant has five main requirements for growth: a certain amount of light, the appropriate-sized pot, the right amount of water, the soil changed regularly, and maintaining a certain temperature. If just one of the five elements is missing, there will be an imbalance, and the plant will struggle to survive. In this way, a relationship also has specific, non-negotiable criteria essential for growth. Relationships, just like plants, are limited by toxic elements. For example, just as no healthy plant could survive being watered with gasoline, no otherwise healthy relationship can thrive with pathological lying. In other words, a relationship can only be as healthy as the unhealthiest behavior in it.

In short, a healthy relationship is one that is not only functional but also thriving. Whereas an unhealthy relationship is one that isn't functioning; it's struggling. I say this because people often think of dysfunctional relationships only in the context of addiction, abuse, and other extremes when, in reality, many less extreme factors can create dysfunction. When a relationship is functional, it runs relatively smoothly.

When a relationship is healthy, the dynamics run smoothly because:

- Both people feel they are being true to themselves or, as some say, being their "authentic selves."

- Both people recognize that conflict will arise from time-to-time in a healthy relationship and they will ensure that the conflict is handled in appropriate and mature ways. They realize that assertive communication means being open, honest, sincere, and solutions-oriented and usually results in both sides feeling closer than before. Yelling, threats, mocking, and so forth are unhealthy, even if both partners are very upset.

- Each partner maintains healthy boundaries and is responsible for their feelings and self-esteem (not continually looking to the other to make them feel loved or good about themselves).

- Both people feel safe, secure, validated, respected, and appreciated.

- Anxiety and resentment are minimal or non-existent.

- Both partners are comfortable sharing their thoughts, feelings, wants, and needs with each other. And even where there is disagreement, there is always respect.

For a relationship to be healthy, these elements have to be true for both partners. If, for example, only one partner uses assertive solutions-oriented communication, but the other is irritably muttering to themselves in response, this isn't healthy. If one partner believes that the issue is resolved while the other is holding a grudge, this isn't healthy.

Here are some more examples of what a healthy relationship looks like versus an unhealthy relationship:

Example #1:

When there is a conflict in an unhealthy relationship, one partner stops talking to the other partner for an indefinite time, causing enormous stress and further damaging the relationship by creating unnecessary anxiety.

When there is conflict in a healthy relationship, one partner tells the other that they are too angry to talk at the moment, but they promise to talk about their concerns and feelings that evening. And then they do.

Example #2:

In an unhealthy relationship, when one partner is frustrated or angry, they lash out at the other, often seeing nothing wrong with their behavior.

In a healthy relationship, both partners know that it's okay to be frustrated or angry, but that it's not okay to treat others with hostility or disrespect.

Example #3:

In an unhealthy relationship, disagreements, crossed boundaries, and hurt feelings are catalysts for teasing, shaming, blaming, and cruel behavior. The goal in a disagreement is to win.

In a healthy relationship, respect and care are always present, especially during disagreements, crossed boundaries, and hurt feelings. The goal in a disagreement is for both people to be heard while feeling safe, secure and assured that they will be treated with dignity and respect, and that the relationship will grow stronger.

Chapter 3: What red flags should I watch out for when dating?

Dear Dana,

I think I'm ready to start dating again, and my friends have recommended I try online dating, but I've also heard a lot of people say to stay away from it because it's full of scammers, predators, and married men looking to cheat. It's been so long since I've been on a date—and I've never met someone off the internet before. I'm feeling overwhelmed by how much has changed since I was in the dating scene. I'm not sure what to do or what to watch out for. Any tips?

~ Kathy

Dear Kathy,

There is a lot of truth that online dating is full of scammers, along with married men and women looking to cheat; however, these types of deceptive people don't only exist online, you can easily come across them in your day-to-day life. Outside of barricading yourself in your house, there is no 100% watertight way to avoid problematic people. All any of us can do is take the necessary precautions, move slowly, keep healthy boundaries, and be okay cutting off contact with people that you don't see yourself having a future with, or with whom things don't feel right for any reason.

One of the ways you can prepare yourself for entering the dating scene is to be as informed as possible about what to expect. The changes you notice that have taken place with dating will depend on your age and experience. If you have been out of the dating scene for at least a decade, your last dating experiences may have involved a man picking you up at your house and the first date being several hours long, involving dinner and a movie or a concert. If you didn't know the man very well, you might have spent quite a bit of time emailing each other or speaking with him on the phone to see if there was enough chemistry before you felt comfortable going on a date. These days, this approach to dating can set you up for failure as well as potentially put you in danger. While the tips in this section are geared towards online dating, many still hold true for dating in general, regardless of where you originally met the person.

Here is some information about online dating:

- According to various studies, less than 1% of people who connect through online dating sites meet in person, so guard your heart and be wary of developing feelings for someone before you've met. In fact, it's essential to go slow, because any feelings you have for this new person are based on the fantasy of who you think they are. The reality of who they are takes time to be seen.

- It's common for people to post either the most flattering, or outdated, pictures of themselves on their profile. So anticipate that the person you meet will look different from their photo.

- Many continue to communicate with a handful of people on dating sites until they feel they want to be monogamous so, again, guard your heart and don't automatically assume that just because you are messaging, or even having sex with someone, that you are in a serious relationship with them. It's vital that, as time goes on, you and the other person have conversations about your relationship to ensure that you both have the same understanding of how serious, or casual, this relationship is.

- There are many deceitful people claiming to be single, divorced, separated, widowed, or in an open marriage when they are actually in a committed relationship or married, so make sure to google their name and pictures. Also, go slow to see if, what I like to call, "squirrely behavior" starts to surface, such as they can't meet or speak during evenings or on weekends, or are evasive about the kind of work they do.

- Some people create a whole fake life on a dating site to boost their self-esteem, see who they can trick, or because they are bored. So you want to make sure you meet them in person sooner rather than later.

- You genuinely don't know the kind of person you are communicating with until you've met them (although, if you get a funny feeling, you don't need to meet them). Even then it takes at least a solid 90 days for people to get comfortable with each other, and to stop being on their best behavior.

- There are different types of chemistry. Your chemistry with someone might seem excellent based on what they've written in their profile, but completely off through emails, texting, phone calls, or in person.

- It's not uncommon for a person to become verbally and emotionally abusive if they are rejected. They may go from being complimentary and kind to rude, insulting, and spew some of the harshest and cruelest things you may have ever heard. This can set a person back in their healing, and I think it's helpful to be aware that this kind of behavior is becoming more frequent.

- Dating is a highly emotional and volatile experience. The process can be an emotional rollercoaster between excitement and exhilaration to disappointment and rejection. For this reason, it's essential to keep your self-worth and hurt feelings in two different buckets to avoid letting any of the negatives impact your self-esteem.

We all think we can spot a scam or dangerous person and, the vast majority of the time, we can't. It's important to realize that no one thinks they will get scammed. This is why it's so important to get familiarized with some of the more common signs of an online scam. One point I want to make clear, however, is that scammers are continually improving and changing their scam. Scammers are also called con (as in "confidence") artists for a reason: people don't fall for scams because they are stupid; they fall for scams because con artists do a great job of building trust and using charm to lure them in. In this section, I mention some of the more common red flags; however, these red flags and the scams themselves will change once the scammers realize that people are onto them.

Signs you are dealing with a scammer:

- Something seems off about their pictures or their level of interest in you. For example, they may be incredibly good-looking, wealthy, young, or their activity level or their interests and hobbies are very different from yours. In short, they may seem out of your league or as though you don't have very much in common with them. In an attempt to smooth over your concerns about differences in age or appearance, they may say that they have a baby face, or look young for their age. Remember, their one profile was created with the intention of hooking hundreds of people.

- Their profile is a little "off." It may have misspellings, strange word choices, or otherwise, seem as though someone who isn't from the area wrote it.

- They will push you to communicate with them off of the dating site, instead of using the email or chat features that the dating site offers. They do this because most dating sites show when the person was last active, and it's hard for scammers to keep up the act that their target is "the only one" if you can see they were active when they weren't talking to you.

- They may claim to have the same religion or religious views or want to take things slow, but their actions say otherwise.

- They will want to communicate with you excessively throughout the day and night. This is done to establish trust and comfort, as well as to create an emotional dependency.

- They will say and do things to gain your trust. For example, they may claim to be in a profession that most people tend to trust, such as the military, health care worker, teacher, or owner of a non-profit. They may claim, or allude to, being financially well-off, such as an entrepreneur, or a successful engineer. The thinking behind this is that a person is more inclined to "loan" money to someone that has the means to pay it back.

- They will say what most people would want to hear, such as how important commitment, family, or religion is to them.

- They say they are a native of your area (regardless of what country you live in) but have a foreign accent once you speak to them on the phone. This isn't to say that everyone who has a foreign accent is a scammer, they aren't. However, many online scammers are operating from outside of the United States. A person having a foreign accent is not necessarily cause for alarm but just a factor to consider along with other factors.

- They may send you a long-stemmed red rose and a small box of chocolates to prove their interest in you. The reason this works is that most people tend to think that scammers wouldn't spend money on their target, that they only ask for money, and this isn't true.

- They may say that their adult child is home from college/ university and wants to speak to you to find out more about who their parent is in love with. The reason they have you talk to another person is to establish additional credibility. Having a third party vouch for what they are saying can be the reassurance of the target needs. After all, a regular, decent person would tend to think that this person they've been communicating with must have sincere intentions if they've told their child about them.

- They may email or text you a picture of an airline ticket to your area to prove that they are coming to visit you.

- Usually, they will have a reason for why they can't meet you in person when the truth is that it is because they are overseas or sending you fake pictures. But don't be misled by this; sometimes a scammer will meet you in person.

- Inevitably, they will ask to borrow money, usually saying that some sort of emergency came up.

- If you are dealing with a person looking for citizenship, they will use charm, and they will push to get married quickly.

The dos and don'ts of online dating:

- Be careful not to create, or fall in love with, a fantasy. If early on you find yourself frequently thinking about a future with them, you are unknowingly creating a fantasy of who they are.

- Do not loan or give money to anyone that you've met online. They will have a compelling story as to why they need the money, but don't fall for it.

- Do not get together with anyone you've met online without letting a trusted person know where you are, who you are with, and how long you plan on being with them.

- Do not let them know where you live and work. Do not give them your last name or phone number. Do not add them as a friend on Facebook or give them any of your other social media profiles. You can't take back this info, and if they are a jerk, obsessive, or creepy, you could find yourself in danger, or, at a minimum, with a bunch of unnecessary stress.

- Do not have them pick you up at your house; meet them in a public place.

- Do not send sexy pictures of yourself. If you do, don't include your face or any identifying tattoos or furniture, as it's common for scammers (and disgruntled exes in general) to use pictures like this for blackmail or to humiliate you. These days, an appropriate degree of caution involves assuming that whatever information you put online, or in a message to someone, will eventually be made public.

- Don't be quick to believe everything a person is telling you. This isn't being paranoid; it's being practical and realistic. Have a healthy degree of skepticism. There are a lot of scammers and predators online.

- I mentioned this before and can't stress it enough: do a google search with any of the personal information they've given you, such as their name, screen name, and photos. You might be surprised by what you find.

- Pay attention to the tone you are setting, or are allowing them to set. As an example if, on the first date, they offer to cook you dinner or suggest watching a movie at their house, this is a common sign that they are looking for sex and are not interested in a relationship.

- When meeting for the first time, make it time restricted (less than two hours, ideally 45 minutes) and during a weekday.

Don't reserve a Friday or Saturday night for a first date with someone, as this sets the tone that you don't have much going on in your life. A simple coffee date works well. The goal here is to see if there is any chemistry because there is nothing more awkward than planning to go out for dinner and a concert only to find, in the first few minutes, that there is no chemistry and you feel uncomfortable around them.

- Avoid talking about any previous relationships for at least the first few months. This is too much information to give to someone right away, and if the relationship ended poorly, it might come across as a red flag to your new date.

- Meet in a public place and let someone know where you are going, who you are meeting, and when you will be home.

- Keep your standards and boundaries healthy, meaning: treat your time, energy, emotions, and body with value.

Remember:

- If a person is looking for a long-term partner, they are going to put in the effort. If they aren't looking for anything serious with you, they will most likely put in the bare minimum needed.

- There is no such thing as a "safe" dating site. Even the ones that charge a monthly membership, or connect people based on their religion, have scammers and predators. There is no substitute for going slow and being cautious.

- Someone looking for sex may deny this yet call you pet names like babe, hon, doll, etc. They may also be overly flirty and make sexual jokes when chatting with you. They could also sign texts with "hugs and kisses" or "xoxo" or "xxxx."

In order to get a feel for how compatible you are with someone, it's essential to go slow and see them in a variety of situations. How do they handle stress, frustration, disagreements, not getting their way? Do they respect your boundaries, or do they try to talk you out of them? Remember, the process of dating is to see if this person makes the right partner for you. So while the dating scene may have changed a great deal in recent times, the ultimate goal has not.

Chapter 4: What are some of the early red flags?

Dear Dana,

I started watching your video series on red flags, and I was shocked by how well you described my experience with my ex. I was wondering if, out of all the red flags that you listed, you could specify some of the early ones?

~ Melissa

Dear Melissa,

While it can be helpful to be aware of the early red flags, it's more important that you learn to become aware of when you feel uncomfortable around someone and how to respond to that when it happens, because it will happen. Those who have encountered an emotionally abusive person, such as a narcissist, tend to be on the lookout for narcissists whose behavior matches what they previously experienced. Though understandable, only looking out for the same type of problematic behavior isn't all that's needed to keep you safe, because if you've met one narcissist, you've met one narcissist, meaning that they are all different. It's vital to remember that every problematic person comes across in their own way. Some yell, threaten, cuss, or are violent, whereas others can come across as incredibly romantic, caring, compassionate, and great listeners. Problematic people come across in such a wide variety of ways that it would be impossible to create a complete list.

For this reason, knowing red flags is only a small part of the solution. The way out of this is to turn inward and get better at acknowledging when you are being treated in a way that isn't okay with you because, too often, survivors are quick to minimize or justify when they are uncomfortable or being mistreated. They second guess themselves and look to others to validate their concerns. If this doesn't happen, they often assume their concerns aren't valid, gloss over them and move full speed ahead.

My point here is that if somebody or something is a problem for you, then it's a problem for you, regardless of what anyone else says and regardless of whether or not it's listed as a red flag. That said, here is just a small sample of "red flags" or some of the ways you can find yourself uncomfortable with someone:

-You may be second-guessing their intentions towards you.

-You simply feel something is "off."

-You find yourself perpetually confused, trying to figure out where a conversation went off track.

-You set a boundary, and they try to talk you out of it. For example, maybe they try to convince you to do something you are uncomfortable doing. Perhaps they push you to share deeply personal things about yourself before you feel ready to share them.

-They want to move the relationship along at a fast pace. Maybe they are professing their love for you before they hardly know you. Perhaps they are talking about moving in together or marriage. They may push for sex sooner than you are comfortable.

Again, this list is far from complete. While many survivors have learned to resist the thrill of a whirlwind romance, the level of emotional intensity can still be tempting to a level that feels intoxicating. Being showered with attention and affection by someone who seems like a soul mate can cause a person to gloss over their concerns and move full speed ahead. It is essential to go slow, make decisions based on your standards, and not look for outside validation if you suspect a person is problematic. While it's possible that a problematic person, even a narcissist, will respect your wish to take things slow, it is unlikely that they will do so for long. A more likely scenario is that your insistence on taking the relationship slowly will mean the narcissist looks elsewhere. A person sincerely interested in you, however, will respect you and your boundaries.

If you don't feel comfortable with something someone is doing, it's crucial that you either address it (depending on what it is) or distance yourself from them. Viewing red flags as early boundary, or standard, pushes can help clear a lot of confusion.

That said, some of the most common early red flags are:

- Disrespecting or arguing about your boundaries

- Attempting to push you into doing something you aren't comfortable with

- Shutting down communication or raging if they don't get their way

- Wanting to talk to you excessively

- Being jealous that others look at you

- Making demands of any kind

- Dictating what you should or shouldn't wear

- Pouting, sulking, or making sarcastic remarks when you do something they don't like

- Wanting you to spend all your time with them and only them

- Coming on fast and telling you everything you want to hear (which is also part of what's known as love bombing)

- Wanting to know deeply personal things about you

- Moving the relationship along at a fast pace, for example, professing their love for you, talking about moving in together, talking about marriage, etc.

When we are in the early stages of a relationship and emotions are running high, it can be easy to rationalize these red flags, or even misinterpret this controlling behavior as caring. If you are in doubt as to what you are experiencing, ask yourself how you would feel if your adult child or good friend were dating someone who treated them like this. Usually, asking yourself that question can give you the clarity you are seeking.

Remember, if you want to get married eventually, then the whole purpose of dating is to see if the other person is what you are looking for in a life partner. Healthy dating involves discernment. It is important that your standards are at such a level that you focus on being choosey, not on being chosen. You are interviewing potential candidates for the most important position in your life. *Red flags aren't missed they are dismissed.* Go slow, assess your level of comfort with a person, validate yourself if you have any concerns (don't look to others to do so), and do not minimize or justify any behavior you find problematic. Red flags can help guide you along the way, but they are not everything, and they are not guaranteed to protect you from harm. Your best protection is your discernment.

Chapter 5: How can I tell if I'm listening to my intuition or being hyper-vigilant?

Dear Dana,

When I look back on my relationship with my abusive ex, I see many red flags. At the time, I remember feeling like something was off with his behavior, but I guess I wanted to give him the benefit of the doubt because I didn't have concrete proof that he was lying. I feel so naive and stupid for glossing over those red flags and for putting up with all of it. What gets me is that I stayed and tried to work on things, but he was the one who ended up leaving me for another woman! I swore to myself that I'd never get into a relationship like that again. The issue I'm dealing with now is that I'm struggling to tell the difference between my intuition and being hyper-vigilant. I feel like everything anyone does is a red flag. Is there a way to know if someone's behavior is an issue or if I'm just overly sensitive and cautious due to my past?

~ Tanya

Dear Tanya,

It's common for someone who has been in an abusive relationship to see red flags in others, making them feel anxious or "crazy." It's common for other people, such as mental health professionals, friends, and family, to discount these red flags as a result of what you went through. However, from my own experience and from listening to the countless experiences of others, I believe there is a good chance that the red flags you are seeing aren't solely related to unprocessed trauma. Instead, they may be the result of an expansion of your awareness of problematic behavior—behavior that you may have rationalized and minimized up until this point.

Hindsight is 20/20, and when, after some time, we look back

on a previous relationship or any problematic situation, we often see many early warning signs. The benefit of hindsight is that we are now more in tune with problematic behavior. The downside is that we may be placing significant pressure on ourselves to identify questionable behavior right from the start. The reality is some problematic behaviors are more evident than others. This can lead to all kinds of insecurity, self-doubt, and uncertainty over whether something is a deal-breaker. We can become an unhinged mess.

Instead of trying to determine the difference between your intuition and hyper-vigilance, switch your focus to what makes you uncomfortable and how to respond to it. Shifting your focus like this eliminates a lot of the mental anguish caused by second-guessing yourself. You don't need to psychoanalyze the person, or your reaction to them, in an attempt to figure out if they are a narcissist, or if their behavior is problematic, or if you are too sensitive. All you need to figure out is how you feel about what you are experiencing. If something someone does is making you uncomfortable, then that's all you need to know.

The next step is figuring out how to handle what you are experiencing. You can distance yourself from the person or address their behavior and see how they handle your concerns. Interaction with others will always fall somewhere on the spectrum of comfortable to uncomfortable. If it's uncomfortable, there's a good chance they've crossed one of your boundaries or have hit on an emotional wound that needs healing. The degree of discomfort we feel often coincides with the degree of the boundary violation that's occurred or is occurring.

When intense emotions surface, it can be challenging to tell the difference between a current boundary violation or unprocessed pain from the past, or even if it's a bit of both.

When you feel an intense emotion, it helps to explore it. Does it feel appropriate for the current circumstances, or does it feel excessive? If someone else had the same reaction from the same situation, would you consider their behavior appropriate or excessive? What I've also found helpful is that the more someone learns about the range of overt and covert forms of verbal, emotional, and psychological abuse, the more clarity and validation they have and are better able to connect their feelings to the event at hand.

For example, without this knowledge, a person may describe their relationship with a co-worker as "tense," but after learning more about dysfunctional behavior will be able to pinpoint why it feels tense. Perhaps the co-worker is dismissive, rude, invalidating, runs hot and cold, and is continually critical of them. Once we have a broader vocabulary about problematic behavior, what was once considered more of a "funny feeling" or even a red flag is now able to be identified as the legitimate concern it is.

Addressing and honoring how you feel rather than asking yourself if you are hyper-vigilant or intuitive doesn't just apply to relationships. It is critical for your overall safety, as well. You may assess a situation, or feel differently about it, then someone else. For example, the other night, my brother and I were walking to the car after leaving a restaurant, and he wanted to take a shortcut through a dark alley. To me, the idea of this was so absurd I thought he was joking. When I realized he was serious, I was shocked by his suggestion, and he was shocked by my refusal. He thought I was overly cautious and paranoid, and I thought he was taking unnecessary risks.

Had this exchange happened ten years ago, my brother's dismissal of my concerns would have sent me into a spiral of self-doubt. I would have second-guessed myself, wondering if he was right, and I was paranoid or overly-cautious. Having always been open and honest with him, I may have debated the issue, pointing out all my reasons for why walking through a dark alley was a bad idea so that he could understand my thinking and then validate me. But not anymore. I've become more comfortable in knowing and asserting my feelings and opinions, and I don't need others to agree with either. This new version of me stood firm in how I felt and asked him to please just humor me and take the lighted route, so we did. Now, had he refused, I would have told him that he could take the alley but that I was going to take the busy, well-lit street and I'd meet him at the car.

Here is another example, this time involving a stranger. I was pet sitting for some friends of mine, and took their dog out for a walk on a sunny Saturday afternoon. I had my headphones in, listening to one of my favorite podcasts when I noticed an older man walking down his driveway towards me. I was startled by this and, at first, thought he must have said something to me that I didn't hear because of my headphones. As he approached, he was making small talk, which was registering as unsettling. Something seemed different than the usual interactions of saying "good morning" to a passing jogger, or stopping so a small child can pet the dog and chatting with their parent, and so forth.

Looking back, I can pinpoint several things that felt concerning: We were on a brisk walk, and he found no issue interrupting it to engage me in small talk. He was standing close to me. He didn't seem interested in the dog. And the angle at which he approached me was from the side, not like a person wanting to engage in conversation. But, at the time, all I knew was that I felt uncomfortable. I tugged on the leash to signal the dog that it was time to go and began resuming my walk.

The man continued trying to engage me in conversation and, again, kept trying to move towards my side, but I told him we needed to get going and wished him a nice day.

Now if this had happened ten years ago, I would have brushed aside my concerns and assumed the man was lonely, perhaps even a widower, and just wanted to talk. I would have shrugged off him approaching me from an odd angle, thinking I was feeling unsettled for no valid reason. I would have let him talk at me while stuffing my discomfort because I didn't want to risk hurting his feelings. I would have allowed my discomfort to grow until he said or did something hurtful or vile, or until he finished talking.

These days I limit uncomfortable situations as much as I can. I feel secure and justified in my boundaries, and don't feel overly responsible for other people's feelings. Was the guy lonely and wanting to talk, or was he looking to say or do something inappropriate or hurtful to me? After all, he was probably in his late 60's, not his 30's, and this was considered a safe neighborhood. I could have easily justified his actions, but the fact is that I didn't need to stand there in an attempt to figure out his intentions. I simply needed to acknowledge how I was feeling in the moment and then take action based on that. Since I felt uncomfortable, I decided to leave. So I did.

Whether we are talking about street smarts or relationship smarts, all you need to do is ask yourself what is unsettling to you? Be honest with yourself. No matter how small or seemingly insignificant something seems to be, no matter what anybody else advises, if it's a problem for you, then it's a problem. That said, it's understandable and appropriate to feel anxious or unsafe (aka experience red flags) around someone who is acting in erratic, inappropriate, concerning, boundary-pushing, dangerous, or otherwise emotionally or physically unsettling ways. We never know someone's real intentions unless they make them known, and by then, a tremendous amount of damage may be done. All we can do is act on how we feel around them, and that's okay.

Because of my own experience with narcissistic abuse, charming, likable men who seemed considerate, caring, and wonderful terrified me. Of course, other people didn't understand this because they thought dangerous people were dangerous looking and, therefore, easy to spot. They didn't know that this is rarely the case and that, more often than not, dangerous people initially come across like Prince or Princess Charming. So what to do when a seemingly great guy induces panic? Well, for a while, I felt more comfortable around men who were overtly problematic because at least I knew what I was dealing with. In short, I was more comfortable with the snake in the street versus the snake in the grass. However, dating jerks as an attempt to stay safe was not the answer.

Before getting tangled up with a charming manipulator, I was mistaking someone being likable for them being a good person. After these experiences, I thought a nice man meant a potentially dangerous man. In reality, a nice man can be either one of those extremes or anywhere on the whole spectrum between them. It took me a long time to figure out how to feel safe with friendly guys. The answer: it was not only okay, but healthy to have a reasonable degree of caution, to go slow, observe their behavior in a variety of situations, address things I took issue with, pay attention to how they responded and, always, to respect whatever I was feeling.

Generally, the concepts of boundaries, standards, and deal-breakers are not taught. In fact, we usually learn the opposite: forgive and forget, be more understanding (because so-and-so had a bad childhood or a bad day), trust others until they break that trust, don't live in the past, be more polite, more tolerant, etc. For reasons like this, it can be challenging to acknowledge, even to ourselves, when we feel uncomfortable around someone. We can feel like we are rude, or like a bad person, for not giving others the benefit of the doubt. We may feel obligated to spend time with a person or give them multiple chances because we don't want to hurt their feelings or be judgmental. If we do otherwise, we might worry that we will lose out on a potentially great relationship. The result of all this is that we silence our concerns and, doing so, cannot see reality. If we allow this social programming to subconsciously drive our behavior we miss out on a fundamental lesson: learning to validate our own instincts instead of seeking validation from others.

Chapter 6: How long can a narcissist keep on their mask?

Dear Dana,

I was married to a verbally and emotionally abusive man for fifteen years. We divorced about five years ago, and I'm just now starting to date again. I've been seeing a wonderful man for the past month; however, I find myself waiting for the abusive side of him to reveal itself. Because of this, I feel like I'm withholding my feelings, so I won't get attached to him if this were to happen. Is there a certain amount of time before a narcissist's mask comes off? When is it safe for me to relax and trust that this man is a decent person?

~ Sam

Dear Sam,

This is one of the top questions that survivors of narcissistic abuse have. For those not familiar with the term: the narcissist's "mask" is the wonderful personality a narcissist often creates to cover their true, abusive nature. It's appropriate and understandable if you've been in an abusive relationship, to be nervous when dating someone new because you know, first-hand, what kinds of people are out there and, worse, that their demeanor can be deceiving. Once survivors start dating again, they find themselves anxious about when their new love interest is going to show an abusive side to themselves. This concern can cause survivors to feel hyper-vigilant, wondering if they will ever be healed, and fearing that they won't.

While the vast majority of the time problematic behavior starts to shine through once the other person doesn't get their way, some can do a great job of being on their best behavior until they feel secure that their partner won't leave—usually, if they live together, are expecting a baby, are in business to-gether, and so on. See what they are like when they don't get their way, when you disagree with them, or set a boundary. Keep in mind, however, that the first few months of any rela-tionship involve an idealized phase where both people are on their best behavior. This stage is often full of romance and passion and feeling as though we've met the perfect person. The fact is that we don't know who they are; we only know who they are on their best behavior when things are going smoothly. Just like a sailor doesn't know their skills until they hit a storm, so too in dating: we don't start to understand who we are dealing with until the weather has changed, and we see how this person acts under pressure.

Currently, you've been dating this man a month, which means that you hardly know him, even though it can feel like you do. You are wise to hold back on falling deeply for this man for those reasons. The only way to see a person for who they are is to take the time to see them in a variety of situations. What are they like, for example, working as a team, handling stress, frustration, or negotiating with others? It's during times like these that a person's level of self-restraint, coping skills, re-spect for others, and ability to problem solve shine through. Stress can bring out the worst in anybody but, even so, it's ap-propriate and reasonable that a stressed person show dignity and respect for others, and handle themselves as maturely as possible so that they don't hurt those around them. Trust in a relationship is largely built by both people handling stressful situations with care and concern for each other.

If both people are honest with their thoughts, feelings, wants, and needs, conflicting points of view will emerge from time-to-time. This is normal and healthy. What matters is how the dispute is resolved. A relationship without conflict isn't healthy; it's a sign of poor communication and that at least one person is engaging in people-pleasing behavior. This passivity eventually results in resentment, which slowly poisons a relationship.

So, while I can't tell you definitively when a narcissist's mask falls off and precisely when you can feel secure with your new relationship, I can recommend that you go slow, that you are assertive when you are being treated in any way that feels bad or uncomfortable, and realize that requiring to be treated with dignity and respect at all times isn't asking for too much; it's the basics of adult behavior.

Chapter 7: I'm tired of dating abusive men. Do you think it's possible for me to talk myself into dating a woman?

Dear Dana,

I'm so tired of being hurt by men that I'm thinking about trying to date women. I'm not gay or bisexual. Is it possible for me to talk myself into being attracted to a woman?

~ Serena

Dear Serena,

I suppose it's possible for you to talk yourself into being attracted to a woman after all lots of things are possible, but whether or not this is a good, or effective, approach to your problem is another story. Having a relationship with a woman won't necessarily keep you safe from abuse as women can be just as abusive as men. Additionally, it would be unfair to the women you date in the same way that you, most likely, wouldn't want to date a gay man who was trying to convince himself, or others, that he was straight and, therefore, was dating you as a perceived solution to some problem.

Let's back things up a bit, as your thought process behind how to stay safe is relatively common, yet problematic. I've come across quite a few women over the years who have been so hurt in relationships with men that they conclude men are the problem, and the solution is to have relationships with women. The thinking behind this tends to be that women, unlike men, are safe and nurturing. My guess is that many women who have a close female friend have joked how if they could only be attracted to each other, then all their dating problems would be solved. Besides trying to force yourself to be sexually attracted to someone you aren't, it's important to know that many women have been shocked and disappointed to find that, contrary to conscious or unconscious stereotypes of femininity, women can be abusive too.

Abusive behavior is the problem and what we need to avoid. Abuse is about power and control over another, and anyone can be abusive. People with abusive behavior exist in all racial and ethnic groups, among all nationalities, gender and sexual identifications, professions, zodiac signs, and socio-economic classes. In short, any human could potentially be an abuser. The smallest kid in the class may be the biggest bully. A five-foot-tall woman may be abusing her 6'4" husband. An eighty-five-year-old grandfather could be abusing his twenty-year-old grandson. The challenge comes in with knowing what problematic behavior is, and seeing it clearly when it surfaces. The world is full of abusive people.

Be honest with yourself when someone's behavior is making you uncomfortable and don't justify their behavior when this happens. Know when to assert yourself, and when their behavior is a deal-breaker and you need to cut off contact. And, finally, do not look to others to agree with the decisions you make because you are the one who has to live with the consequences. Second-guessing your concerns, or ignoring them, is like turning down the volume on your GPS when it is telling you to turn around because you believe it is mistaken. If we only start to listen to the GPS once we are in a ditch, this is a problem. In the same way it is important to heed your own internal GPS when it starts talking to you. This is the most powerful way to avoid abusive relationships.

Chapter 8: When do I tell my new partner about my abusive ex?

Dear Dana,

I've been dating this new guy for a few weeks, and he's terrific, but I find myself pulling back and being fearful of him flipping a switch like my ex did and then becoming abusive. He senses my hesitation and keeps asking me what's wrong, but I don't want to scare him off with the horror story that was my previous relationship. When should I tell my new partner about my abusive ex?

~ Alan

Dear Alan,

I can understand why you would want to tell your new partner about the abuse you endured, so he will, hopefully, better understand the root cause of much of your anxiety. I can also understand why you would be hesitant to open up about what happened because those who haven't experienced abuse may not understand it, and may view us in a negative light or ask insensitive questions. While I do think it is important for you to tell your new partner what you experienced, I encourage you to wait until the relationship has more time to develop before you begin opening up. The reason is that the relationship is still very new, and a substantial level of emotional safety and trust hasn't had a chance to grow yet.

Opening up to someone about sensitive parts of your past too soon can make one feel overly exposed after the fact, and it may be too much personal information. I would wait until you decide that this relationship has long-term potential and a substantial degree of trust that has been established before exposing these wounds to him, as you will need for him to handle them appropriately or you run the risk of feeling re-victimized by his lack of understanding.

The problem isn't that you want to pull back, the problem is that you are not ready to move full speed and are in conflict with over this. You can't make yourself feel more secure in this relationship; only time can do that. Pulling back is probably a good thing as a few weeks of spending time with someone isn't enough for a relationship to form yet. Right now, there are only two people focused on what they have in common and sexual attraction is probably high. These two elements are significant, but they are only part of what makes for a relationship. For these reasons, I don't view pulling back as a problem. I see it as you finding balance. If, for example, you are spending every day with him and pulling back means you spend three or four days with him instead, this is a good thing, especially if that time away from him is spent with your friends, engaging in your hobbies or otherwise nurturing your own life so that he doesn't become your whole world.

In addition to opening up slowly as the relationship grows, you also want to make sure you aren't turning him into your therapist or looking for him to heal you. His understanding can only go so far, as he wasn't the one who experienced the trauma. For this reason, finding a therapist who specializes in trauma or abusive relationship can help you to work through these feelings.

Additionally, it's important to note that if early on, you are having concerns about this new partner, that you address those concerns. During the next few months, take notice of how he behaves in a wide range of situations—especially when he gets upset, frustrated, or irritated. Make a mental note of how he handles other details about your life that are sensitive to you. When a person acts appropriately in situations like this, emotional safety is cultivated. In addition, prepare yourself for the possibility that he may not know how to handle this information, as most people don't. For example, it's not uncommon for people to respond to news like this by trying to make light of things, telling insensitive jokes, or getting defensive, thinking that you are fearful they might be abusive.

When you do decide that the time is right to start opening up about your ex, I encourage you to do so a little at a time so that you can see how he handles the information and then determine if you feel safe sharing more. If you have worked through a lot of the pain of this previous relationship, then it can be helpful to tell him that you don't want to bring the past into your present relationship. Saying something like this can give your partner the reassurance that he needs that you are ready to be in a new relationship.

Because most people who have never experienced abuse don't know what to say to something like this, you might want to start by saying, "I wanted to share with you a bit about why I'm so anxious. I don't want to go into great detail, but suffice it to say that my ex had two very different sides to himself. He could be charming and seemingly considerate, and he could also be very manipulative and cruel. The result is that I find myself feeling anxious around new people, wondering if they might be the same way. My guess is that I won't experience anxiety at this level once I get to know you better, and I hope it won't get in the way of the relationship we are building."

If, at any time after this conversation for any reason, he defends or minimizes your former partner's actions, blames you, gets irritated or shifts the blame to your past, this is a problem either worth addressing or ending the relationship over if you so choose. If even in the absence of those more problematic responses, he is simply not as supportive as you were hoping, at a minimum, this is a sign to pull back on opening up further about the abuse. He will need to prove that he is able to be supportive and respectful when you allow yourself to be vulnerable with him.

Depending on how much you've been able to work through what happened, when you do share, you could let him know matter-of-factly. Doing so can help him realize that you have transitioned from survivor to thriver—someone who has gained insight and learned valuable lessons, and that you are not wanting or needing not to rehash everything that happened. Talking with him about it in this way lets him know that the abusive relationship is not *the* defining event in your life, it's just *an* event in your life, although some residual anxiety still exists.

Chapter 9: How will I know when I'm ready to date again?

Dear Dana,

It's been two years since the relationship with my emotionally abusive ex ended. I've tried going on a few dates here and there but didn't feel ready. How will I know when I'm ready to date again?

~ Carmen

Dear Carmen,

I hear a lot of people say that, if a person is anxious about dating, or still fears being abused, then they aren't ready to date. I disagree with this. Odds are you will always feel some degree of anxiety when it comes to dating, and you may still find yourself concerned that the person you are dating could be abusive. To a certain degree, these feelings are normal after abuse. Just like if you were in a traumatic car accident, you may, from time-to-time, feel a little nervous being in a car or traffic. This is understandable given what happened before. Trying to get rid of all anxiety is most likely going to, ironically, cause you more anxiety when some degree of stress resurfaces. It's more the degree and frequency of the anxiety that is the larger issue, but let's focus on the dating component of your question.

Being ready to date entails quite a few things. Here are ten key signs that you are ready:

1. You believe that you have value. You wholeheartedly believe that being treated with dignity and respect is a fundamental human right and not something you need to earn in a relationship. You must believe that you have value in order to feel you are worthy of protecting. This includes having functional

boundaries, standards, and deal-breakers necessary for forming fulfilling, nourishing relationships and leaving those that aren't.

2. You know how to value yourself: your time, energy, emotions, body, and environment. Knowing you have value and treating yourself as though you have value are, strangely enough, two different things. You don't hope, argue with, or try to convince others to treat you with value and respect you; you insist upon it through having functional boundaries, standards, and deal-breakers.

3. You understand that love or lust are not reliable criteria on which to make a decision about a life partner. Additionally, being in love with someone isn't a valid reason to stay in a toxic situation. The foundational components of a workable relationship are, instead, based in good character, the ability to negotiate, work as a team, and communicate in a functional way. These are the factors that create an emotionally stable and safe environment in which both people can grow.

4. You know when you are being treated in a way that makes you uncomfortable and that, when this happens, you either need to be assertive or get some distance from the person.

5. You understand that you are in charge of your life. You might ask others for advice, but you don't let their opinion sway you into taking actions that don't feel right to you.

6. You no longer wait for concrete proof that a situation is problematic. Instead, you release the need to wait around for things to get worse because you realize that any dynamic that feels perpetually "off," chronically confusing or crazy-making, causing mental anguish, or that cannot be resolved, isn't worth being in.

7. You are choosey when it comes to the criteria you have for

a partner; you aren't focused on being chosen. You know your value, and if others don't appreciate it, then you aren't going to waste time proving it to them; you may have hurt feelings, but these don't spill over into negatively impacting your self-worth. You aren't starved out for attention or affection, and you are meeting your own wants and needs in life. Dating is a process of discernment where you are seeing if this other person has the qualities you are looking for in a partner. Instead of being flattered that they are interested in you, focus on asking yourself if they are right for you.

8. You feel confident setting the pace of the relationship and going slow. You are able to keep yourself from becoming emotionally invested in someone right away.

9. You have built up a life that you love and, as a result, you are dating from a place of wholeness, not from a space of looking for another person to "complete" you. Because of this, you won't be excessively emotionally reliant on the other person (a codependent relationship).

10. You do not look for a partner or being in a relationship to heal you. The process of dating is full of rejection. If being rejected is going to send you to a dark place emotionally, it is best you first build up your life (hobbies, social life, support system, etc.) Granted, there is only so much healing a person can do on their own, as many unhealed emotional wounds only become painful once they could be "touched" again. Your mental and emotional health is your responsibility, and you are worth making this a priority in your life. If you have functional communication with a "healthy enough" partner, then each person's wounds can be discussed, and additional healing can occur. This can be rocky terrain to navigate, so for more information, please visit: www.thriveafterabuse.com/healing-in-a-relationship

Chapter 10: Is it a problem if the person I'm dating wants me to look a certain way?

Dear Dana,

I recently met this guy on a dating website. We exchanged about a dozen or so pictures and planned to meet. He messaged me, asking if I was a "girly-girl" and that he is only attracted to women who wear makeup and heels. I was a little taken aback by his comment but chalked it up to some of the photos I'd sent him where I guess I might have looked like a tomboy (I was camping). I thought it was a little weird that he was telling me what he liked women to wear. For our first date, I made sure to wear a dress and heels. We went out for dinner and had a decent time; however, by the end of the night, I could barely walk my feet hurt so bad. He called me the next day and said that he'd like to take me out to dinner again that night. I showed up wearing dressy jeans and much lower heels, explaining that I overdid it the night before and needed to give my feet a break. He got upset with me for "not putting more effort into" my appearance. His comment shocked me, as it's not like I was dressed like a slob. I was dressed like most of the other women in the restaurant. I told him that he was rude, and he got upset and told me I had lied to him and was using him to get free meals. During dinner, he would hardly speak to me, and we left soon after we ate. He texted me the next day telling me that he thinks we have potential as a couple, but only if I am ready to apologize and agree to show up to future dates "looking like a lady." His response threw me for a loop. Am I over-reacting for having issues with him telling me what I should and shouldn't wear?

~ Amanda

Dear Amanda,

No, you aren't over-reacting to his behavior, and yes, it's concerning how "insistent" (controlling) he was about your appearance as well as how rude and inappropriate he was to bring it up. Additionally, his lack of empathy regarding your sore feet is concerning. It sounds like this man was looking for a submissive piece of arm candy.

While we all have our preferences for what we are attracted to and how we like our partner to look and act, this man has more than preferences; he has expectations. And his expectations are rigid, narcissistic, and not the dynamic you are looking for. Keep in mind that these were only your first couple of dates when people are usually focused on making a good impression, not trying to control the other. If this is how this man acts right out of the gate, then things are only going to worsen.

But let's back up a bit because there is a lot to examine from your brief experience with this guy. One of the biggest challenges survivors of abuse have when it comes to dating, and interacting with other people in general, is knowing when their boundaries are being violated and how to handle that. Many survivors justify, or gloss over, being mistreated and give a person with problematic behavior the benefit of the doubt. Unintentionally, this then lets the problematic person set the pace and tone of the relationship. If we aren't sure when a boundary is crossed, then the odds of us keeping hurtful people in our lives is high. You did a great job with asserting yourself and making it clear that you are an adult and don't want someone telling you what to wear. When he responded the next day acting as if you were in the wrong and the one with the outrageous behavior, he was planting seeds of doubt within you.

So let's dig deeper and go through some less obvious red flags or points of concern. When he told you that he was only attracted to "girly girls" and so forth, we know you found his comment problematic because you said that you were taken aback by it—and that's all we need to know. For you, he crossed a line, even though it might seem like a small one. We don't need to psychoanalyze him or get into a debate about the femininity of women, or if he's right or wrong for having preferences. All we need to know is that what he said registered as a little off-putting for you. This is an excellent example of a boundary being crossed.

Asserting yourself in this situation could have meant saying something like "I don't find this conversation appropriate" or telling him that you wear a variety of clothing styles depending on the situation, or canceling the date if you weren't interested. What concerns me is that you gave him the benefit of the doubt and went out on a date, dressed in a way that pleased him, but not you. In doing this, you gave him a lot of control regarding your appearance and were, perhaps, more focused on getting his approval rather than determining if he was the kind of man with whom you wanted to be in a relationship. Learning to recognize your boundaries, and getting comfortable with asserting yourself, takes time and practice. Being uncomfortable with how you are being treated is enough of a reason to either address it with the person who caused the discomfort, or distance yourself from that person. And it doesn't matter what anybody else thinks.

Chapter 11: How can I enjoy dating a boring guy when my ex's love bombing had been so exciting?

Dear Dana,

My therapist said that I'm attracted to men that are charming and attentive—love bombers—and that I need to date a boring guy. My problem is that I'm not attracted to boring men. I'm really drawn to all of the romance that comes with love bombing but, at the same time, I know that love bombers often reveal themselves to be manipulative and abusive. Is there a way for me to stop being attracted to love bombing and to date a boring guy?

~ Katie

Dear Katie,

The reason love bombing is so enticing is that it can feel good to be "bombed" with attention and affection—especially if someone has been walking around feeling unloved, unimportant, or lonely. When someone says and does everything a person needs, it can feel like they have met their perfect partner.

The concept of love bombing was initially used to describe the intensity and persistence that cults use to recruit new members. Love bombing can be either intentional or unintentional. After all, most people in cults don't realize they are in one, and usually when they try and recruit others to join, there isn't malicious intent. They believe in what their group offers and, having been love bombed themselves, are bathed in feel-good hormones such as dopamine, oxytocin, and serotonin, which creates a sense of euphoria—they genuinely want others to experience this for themselves, not realizing that they are persuading loved ones to do something damaging. We all feel this way when we experience something that seems like the answer we've been looking for.

For the malicious manipulators out there in the dating world, love bombing is a weapon used to lure the target in by "bombing" them with endless attention and affections. This often includes compliments, gifts, discovering all kinds of things in common, telling you everything you want to hear, convincing you that you are soul mates, and so forth. This is so enticing, so hard to resist because it can feel good, to say the least, to be "bombed" with such attention and affection—but, in time, problematic behavior surfaces, and the love-bombing becomes the sweet talk needed to keep the target around.

While love bombing is contrived, most relationships, whether they end up being abusive or not, start with a fantasy or idealize stage that can look like love bombing, where each person wears the proverbial "rose-colored glasses" and thinks the other is amazing. They, for example, may create pet names for each other, spend hours talking or texting, and focus on everything they have in common. While this is common, it's important to realize that this is a stage, it doesn't last, and is based on the fantasy each person has of the other before they know each other well. In mature, healthy relationships, both people realize this stage is a passionate, and somewhat fun, whirlwind. However, they know it's temporary and look forward to this phase ending so they can start to assess whether or not this connection is on solid ground. This is why it's important to go slow, making sure that a stable foundation emerges based on healthy communication, character, commitment, and overall chemistry.

This doesn't mean that you need to date a boring guy. This means that the adjustment needs to be made to see the romantic whirlwind as temporary and not something that lasts. Once you start to see either love bombing, or the fantasy stage, as only temporary, it should lose much of its appeal to you. Love bombing turns the volume way up on the fantasy stage. It can be challenging to slow down or walk away when someone tells you everything you want to hear. Don't mistake the love bomber's intensity for sincerity or chemistry. Best-case scenario you are experiencing the idealize stage and worst-case scenario, it's a malicious and appealing illusion the love bomber is creating.

When people speak about dating a "boring" person, they are usually referring to someone who has predictable behavior versus a manipulative or abusive person who often has intense, hot-and-cold type of response. These hot and cold extremes can easily be confused for love and passion (as many movies, TV shows, and songs promote this idea) because the hot times are full of connection, but the cold times are hurtful. These ups and downs are an emotional roller coaster, with attention and affection given in abundance, and then taken away as punishment or, sometimes, seemingly for no reason at all. The person on the receiving end then becomes desperate to do whatever it takes to get the love and security of the relationship back again. People with abusive behavior also tend to come across as very persistent, whether they are trying to win over somebody for the first time, or if they are trying to get them back into the relationship. This persistence isn't love, it's control, and it's a game they are playing.

Once you see this kind of behavior as the emotionally unsafe and exhausting roller coaster that it is, it will lose much of its appeal. It's much easier to avoid getting caught up in the intensity of love bombing when you see it as temporary, and either infatuation or outright manipulation. With this change in perspective, consistent, mature behavior will, in time, start to be more attractive. This doesn't mean that you have to get into a boring routine with someone, it just means that you enjoy being in a stable relationship, not one full of intensity with flowery promises and sweet talk.

Chapter 12: How can I tell if something is a problem or if I'm overreacting?

Dear Dana,

I see some red flags in my new partner, but I don't want to overreact and potentially lose a great relationship. How can I tell if I'm too sensitive or if what I am experiencing is a problem?

~ Jo

Dear Jo,

When we experience red flags, we are experiencing something that we aren't comfortable with. Someone's behavior may strike us as odd, inappropriate, suspicious, or confusing, or perhaps they've crossed one of our boundaries. All red flags, whatever they may be, require our attention and action. Usually, the result is that we either need to assert ourselves and draw a clear boundary, or we need to get some emotional and/or physical distance.

The concept of a red flag can be somewhat confusing as people tend to think of a red flag as majorly problematic behavior, and so get caught up trying to determine if what they are experiencing is, in fact, a big problem. This kind of thinking leads to inaction and staying in a problematic situation until there is concrete proof of a problem, which, by then, is usually so big a tremendous amount of damage has been done. One of the main reasons people stay in this holding pattern while a problem grows, is that they fear voicing their concerns would result in them losing out on a great relationship, opportunity, or situation. Instead, they stay, all the while trying to suppress their discomfort and uncertainty, fearing, yet subconsciously hoping, that they are the one with the issue.

The reason this is done is because if the issue is with them then they have the ability to change, but if the issue is with the other person then there's not much they can do other than to leave the relationship—which they don't want to do.

I find it helpful to swap out the words "red flag" for "uncomfortable behavior" because a red flag is only a signal that something isn't sitting right with you. *Red flags aren't seen, they are felt.* You don't need to wait for further proof to address the situation. If you are experiencing confusion and uneasiness about your partner's behavior, then a conversation that leads to a resolution is necessary. This is because any situation that results in perpetual mental anguish isn't good for your health and the relationship isn't able to grow during this time. When uncertainty is present, trust is not. If no trust is present in a relationship, then feeling safe and secure isn't possible, and chronic anxiety, depression, and insecurity will result.

For these reasons, there is no reason to try and differentiate between a little or big red flag. *Any concern is valid, no matter how small, and has the potential to destroy a relationship if left unresolved.* When people talk about big red flags, what they usually mean is that what they are experiencing is more than a concern; it's a deal-breaker.

So let's distinguish between red flags and deal-breakers. Everyone determines for themselves what their deal-breakers are, but common examples would be: abuse of any kind, active addictions, and adultery. If you sense anything like this going on, you do not need concrete proof that they are, in fact, abusing, using, or cheating. The lack of trust and the inability for your concerns to be addressed and resolved in an appropriate way is all of the concrete proof you need, as this type of dynamic isn't workable.

Red flags are more like flashes of inappropriate or concerning behavior that often build up over time to become deal-breakers. To see a red flag for what it is, we must be able to be honest with ourselves when we experience something concerning and not offer up justifications or excuses. In terms of relationships, it is essential to be able to connect your boundaries being crossed with being treated in a way that you aren't comfortable with. In order to address this misstep or violation, we have to first be aware that it's occurred.

People who have been in one abusive relationship, regardless of the type of abuse they experience, are prone to being in multiple abusive relationships. One of the reasons for this is that they are quick to give others the benefit of the doubt. They are also likely to silence whatever concerns they may have because they know that, especially when dating, they generally tend to feel uneasy and suspicious. They may gloss over these red flags thinking that they are the ones with issues due to their previous relationships. Brushing aside concerns is understandable if a person feels like they are hyper-vigilant, and everything anyone does feels like a red flag; or if others around them offer up justification for why a particular behavior is perfectly fine. Self-doubt or doubt planted by others doesn't help—it just gets a person further away from trusting themselves.

If you determine that a red flag does not immediately fall into your deal-breaker behavior, then address it with the person and pay attention to how they handle your concern. Do they minimize it, or take it seriously? Do they spin the conversation around to talk about issues that they have with you? Do they sulk, get defensive, or give the silent treatment? Do they seem genuine about your concern but then continue with the behavior anyway? *How someone handles your concern, or a conflict, is as important as the concern, or conflict at issue, itself.* If issues are brought up and not resolved, communication isn't the issue; the problem is a lack of sincere interest or sustained motivation by the other person to change.

Keep in mind that what is concerning, or a red flag, varies from person to person. For example, I would find it uncomfortable if a person I recently started dating asked to borrow money, couldn't hold a job, had a quick temper, or needed to drink alcohol to relax or have fun. Other people might not see this kind of behavior as concerning, and that's okay. My life, just like your life, is not a democracy, and we don't need to take a vote to decide what is, or is not, concerning. If something is a problem for you, then it's a problem; others don't need to agree.

We all take issues with different things, I don't think anyone is "too sensitive" as each of us are bothered by different things at different times. For example, someone might make a joke about another person's cooking. If the cook doesn't find it funny, then this doesn't mean that the cook is too sensitive, this means that they don't think the joke is funny. It doesn't matter whether the other person intentionally tried to hurt the cook's feelings. What can hurt someone's feelings, or upset them, varies from person-to-person. Each person has the right to feel the way they do; this is why making your boundaries known is so vital. But realize that it's also okay to distance yourself if you consider their behavior so problematic that it's not worth the battle that would ensue to make the relationship workable. As it is, behavior that you consider this problematic would also be behavior indicating a significant mindset difference from your own, which is a major incompatibility anyway.

For this reason, while being assertive and addressing concerns is essential, it's equally important to know when to walk away. Breakdowns in communication are not the root of every relationship issue. If you find yourself continually addressing, or explaining, the basics of appropriate behavior, then it's time to think about walking away. Remember, the whole point of dating is to see if you have compatibility across all the important areas of life, not trying to get another person to change.

Chapter 13: How can I be sure that this guy was a narcissist?

Dear Dana,

I feel like I'm still learning to spot red flags and set boundaries. After things ended with my abusive ex, I dated this other guy for three months, and things seemed to be going great until he ghosted me. It really rattles me to think I could have been dating another jerk for three months and didn't realize it. I would never get back with him, but I can't help but wonder if this guy was a narcissist. What do you think?

~ Melissa

Dear Melissa,

Most, if not all, relationships start with some degree of an "idealize" or honeymoon phase where things are, well, ideal. The infatuation or fantasy part of a relationship isn't real, but it sure can feel like it--and worse, it can feel like the healthiest, most amazing relationship you've ever been in. During this time, both people are on their best behavior and putting in more effort than they would typically, similar to how someone behaves during a job interview and the first few months after they are hired. Once both people start becoming more comfortable around each other, the fantasy ends, and the reality begins. Each person settles in, and different facets of their personality begin to surface.

The challenge with the idealize stage is that it feels so perfect and wonderful that, if we don't see it as a fantasy, we will forever chase this stage in hopes of getting it back. So while the first three months were wonderful for you, I'm sorry to say that it doesn't sound like they meant that much to him. When a relationship goes from hot to cold like this, it can be confusing and hurtful. It's hard to say what happened here, other than some people, intentionally or unintentionally, can find or create great chemistry with others. If he's one of those people, then everyone he spends time with leaves feeling this deep connection with him.

I've seen survivors of abuse, time and again, try to understand the behavior of others in a piece-by-piece kind of way, asking questions such as, "Is this an example of his mask slipping?" "Is this love bombing?" "Is this person a narcissist?" Trying to figure out the behavior of others like this often leads to more confusion than clarity. The kicker is that regardless of whether or not a person's behavior fits a definition, or even what others say—it doesn't matter. What matters is how you feel about how you are being treated.

Chapter 14: How do I go about dating and trusting men again?

Dear Dana,

Three years ago, my now ex-husband left me out of the blue the day before my birthday, saying that he couldn't handle my jealousy and insecurity anymore. Over the past few months, I saw that he was Facebook friends with several women and was taking his phone with him everywhere, even sleeping with it under his pillow. When I asked him about all this, he became enraged and moved out that night. I didn't think I was jealous and insecure; I just wanted an answer. About a week or so after he left, I found out that he had profiles on multiple dating sites, claiming that he was looking for "the one" and that he was tired of being single!

I was floored. We'd been together for five years, and I'd always thought we had this fantastic relationship. We talked about everything (or so I thought), and we spent the vast majority of our time together. Gradually, I found out that he was living a double life the whole time we were together, which included numerous affairs. And he lied about almost everything. He told me he was in law school, that he'd never been married before, and that his mother had died in a car accident when he was a child. Dana, none of this was true.

I am scared that I will never recover from this and that there are no decent men out there. At some point, I do eventually want to get married and have children. But he hurt me at a level I didn't know was possible. How do I ever trust a man, let alone date again?

~ Eve

Dear Eve,

Over the years, I've found that certain questions tend to be asked more often than others. Your question of, "How can I trust again?" is one of those. And what people usually mean by the question is "How do I go back to trusting people as I did before?" or "How do I go back to instantly trusting and taking people at face value?" My answer is: you don't. Most of us, myself included, have had the thinking that the healthy, reasonable thing to do is to give someone our trust until they break it. And, for the vast majority of the time, this thinking worked because the vast majority of people out there are decent people. However, giving the wrong people our trust can have catastrophic consequences.

So how do we walk the line between being trusting and staying safe? Well, I think that's done by realizing that *trust isn't blindly given, it's earned, and it's built over time by someone exhibiting trustworthy behavior.*

The best example I've ever heard of how trust is built is in Brene Brown's book, *Daring Greatly* where she tells the story of a marble jar that her son's teacher used as a way to track the class' good behavior. The teacher had a decent-sized marble jar that she would drop one marble into each time the class was behaving, and, consequently, would take one marble out of each time the class was misbehaving. Once the jar was full, the class was rewarded with a pizza party. Filling that jar took the class behaving appropriately over enough time; there was no rushing the process. The same concept goes for building trust with others.

When we see appropriate actions, we drop a metaphorical marble in our marble jar. If something a little concerning happens, we take a marble out. And sometimes they might do one thing that is so problematic (cheating or abusing for example) that we need to dump the whole jar and walk away. For someone to fill up their jar, we have to see them in a variety of situations, which takes time.

Normal, decent people frequently assume that others are like them. Because of this, they confuse the niceness in others for goodness or trustworthiness. Doing so is a mistake, and one that you, I, and countless others have learned the hard way, and one on which the problematic people of the world are relying. We have to go slow when getting to know others, as we all think that we can spot a problematic person, but most of the time, we are wrong. It's easy to spot the wolves in wolves' clothing; however, it's the wolves in sheep's clothing that are the biggest concern. These types of people often come across as incredibly charming, nice, and like the ideal partner. If they didn't come across like this, they wouldn't be as effective at manipulating people.

Going slow getting to know someone isn't about being overly cautious or suspicious; it's about being careful and taking our time with who we let into our inner circle. When we do this, we respect ourselves, our time, and our emotions as moving quickly, before we get to know a person, puts us in an unnecessarily vulnerable position.

So could you go slowly with getting to know a new man, only to have him leave or radically violate your trust? Yes. Because people are unpredictable and things happen; however, going slow, and not getting emotionally involved right away, will dramatically improve the odds that trust earned is trust well-placed.

Keep in mind that while there is no shortage of problematic people out there, there is also no shortage of really great people out there too. Take your time with meeting new people, and triple up on your self-care right now. You've been through a lot, and it's a good idea to take some time to recover before you consider dating again.

Chapter 15: Is it possible for someone to fall in love almost immediately after having met?

Dear Dana,

Is it possible for someone to believe they are falling in love almost immediately after having met? We've gone on four dates. I've told him that's way too fast for me, and he said he's okay with that but that he's ready for us to be in a serious relationship as soon as I'm ready. I'm the first person he's dated since his fiancé passed unexpectedly (I saw pictures of her on Facebook), which was pretty tragic. So part of me understands that he might have a life-is-short-don't-waste-time mentality. But the other part of me says this is not normal at all. I'm not saying he's abusive, but is falling in love this fast even possible, or is it a "red flag," something I need to run from?

~ Shelly

Dear Shelly,

Many things are possible; however, I think the bigger question here is how deep can a person's love for someone possibly be if they hardly know them? The answer is that it can't be very deep at all. Love isn't just a feeling; it's also actions that reveal themselves repeatedly over time. It's treating a person with appreciation, dignity, and respect in a wide variety of ways. Strong feelings expressed by somebody you've only been on four dates with are part of the infatuation stage, which occurs at the beginning of almost all relationships.

In other words, because he hasn't known you long enough, his feelings are based on a fantasy of who he thinks you are, not the reality. This infatuation phase tends to last for a few months and then progresses into the "negotiation" phase. The negotiation phase is where both people start becoming more relaxed within the relationship and, because of this, aren't so eager to impress. They feel more comfortable disagreeing and sharing their real opinions. During this time, it's essential to see how each person handles confrontation and conflict, and if issues can be resolved.

So, regardless of how in love and committed he says he is, irrespective of how much chemistry you both may feel, I think it's more important for you to take the time to figure out if he is what you are looking for rather than if he is really in love with you. There can be many reasons, not all of them manipulative, for why people may want to rush into a relationship. But, even if those reasons don't have a toxic source, it remains wise to go slow.

Besides honesty and respect, a stable relationship starts with a solid foundation of open, sincere, solutions-oriented communication. You want to experience how he speaks and acts in as wide a variety of situations as possible. You want to gain an understanding of how he thinks. What are his morals and values? What are his relationships like with those in his inner circle? How well do these things mesh with where you see your life? How does he handle anger, hurt feelings, frustration, and the boundaries of others? Do the two of you have core things in common? These questions are only a small part of what is involved in deeply getting to know someone. Getting to know someone to the point where you genuinely love them and are ready to make it a committed relationship, takes time.

Chapter 16: I feel like I'm always holding my breath when I meet new people, is this normal?

Dear Dana,

I feel like I'm always holding my breath when I meet new people—like I'm waiting for something terrible to happen, or waiting for them to reveal that they are toxic. What is wrong with me?

~ Vanessa

Dear Vanessa,

This level of anxiety is normal after a person has experienced abuse; however, hopefully, by the end of reading this, you'll be able to let go of some of this fear and replace it with a healthy degree of caution. In an attempt to illustrate my point, let me tell you a story about Simon, an adorable little dog I once owned. Simon was a corgi-chihuahua mix and looked like a small smiling sausage. Kids loved him; however, he didn't love kids. Even though he seemed harmless, he was far from it. He was a rescue dog and had a rough past that left him very skittish, with a long history of nipping and biting people—especially children. When we would go for walks, I was surprised by the number of children, and their parents, who instantly let their guard down around him because he was small and cute. If someone hasn't been bitten by a friendly-looking dog before, they might think that they could immediately tell a dog that was going to bite from one who wasn't. And they would be wrong.

If we haven't been bitten by a harmless-looking dog, we may assume—much like those parents and children—that cute, little dogs are harmless. And people who've never been bitten before tend to think that those who are cautious around dogs are naturally uptight, but they aren't. Anybody who has experience being around enough animals understands that they are all different and that not all dogs who are going to bite are big, mean-looking, snarling, and growling. Sometimes a small, smiling dog can get startled and bite for no reason whatsoever. Those who have been bitten may find themselves a little hesitant around dogs, as they should be. Dogs, like people, are all different, and we can't tell just by looking at them if they are friendly. A healthy degree of caution is always appropriate until we know how they will interact with us.

After a situation like this happens, it's common for someone to feel a little nervous around all dogs, fearing that the dog may bite them at any time, because they are now aware a hurtful dog or, for our purposes, person can't always be spotted ahead of time. Because we are now cautious and alert, this change in our behavior can be upsetting, and we might find ourselves wishing we could go back to that carefree person we used to be. But life doesn't work like that—and this is a good thing because if it did, we wouldn't be learning some really important lessons.

Let's extend the example of being bit by a dog a little more, as being bit by a dog and being in an abusive relationship actually have quite a lot in common not only with our own reactions to these experiences but from the reactions of others as well. We notice that we are uncomfortable around dogs when we weren't before, and we don't like feeling this way. We want to go back to the way we used to feel around them. And when we tell other people that dogs now make us nervous, they may tell us that getting bit was a fluke and that it won't happen again, so don't hold it against all dogs. And so we try to do precisely that, but we can't shake the anxiety.

Like I mentioned before, dogs, like people, are all different, so we can't automatically assume someone is harmless based on appearances. So, considering that there are hurtful people out there, you are wise to take some precautions. The biggest one is knowing when you are treated in a way that is not okay with you, so you can set boundaries and assert yourself when somebody crosses a line. Some boundaries are more relative to one's culture than others, such as the understanding of appropriate personal space, eye contact, or touch. However, for the most part, other people do not know where your boundaries are, so it's important to make them known. It's important not to minimize or justify any behavior you find problematic. Rationalizing our concerns is what many of us did while in an abusive relationships and, maybe, have continued to do in other problematic dynamics. You will come across all kinds of people throughout your life, and time will show you everything that you need to know about them, it's up to you as to how to respond.

On the other hand, some survivors believe that the abusive person in their life was a fluke and that the odds of getting tangled up with someone like that again is slim. The result is that once enough time has passed, they either go back to (or pressure themselves into) their old ways of immediately trusting others. What survivors need to know is that, instead of immediately dropping our guard and becoming emotionally involved in a new person, we need to take a few steps back, realizing that trust is earned with appropriate behavior over time. Not only is it understandable, but it is also healthy to have a reasonable degree of caution when getting to know new people.

Chapter 17: How can I tell what should be a deal-breaker, and what is workable?

Dear Dana,

I'm several years out of the relationship with my abusive ex. I've done a lot of healing and feel like my boundaries are much better these days; however, I still struggle with telling the difference between what's a deal-breaker and what's workable. I find myself either giving a person too many chances or cutting them out of my life immediately. For example, I went on a handful of dates with one guy who was chronically late. He always had a different reason for why this was, and so I kept seeing him. I later found out he was married and had three kids, which is why he could never commit to a time. Or, on the other hand, if, after a few dates, if I've see a man become rude or demanding, I cut things off immediately. When this has happened, other people tell me that I'm over-reacting by ending things right away. I guess what I'm asking is, is there a way to determine what a reasonable deal-breaker is and what should be workable behavior?

~ Lisa

Dear Lisa,

When it comes to discerning what "should" be deal-break-er behavior or workable behavior, it's not about telling the difference between them. What's important is that you can determine what works or doesn't work for you, what you feel is worth discussing, and how long you are willing to wait for certain behaviors to change. There's an old Kenny Rogers song called "The Gambler" that sums this process up well. It goes, "You gotta know when to hold 'em, know when to fold 'em, know when to walk away, and when to run." Un-fortunately, that level of discernment, with playing poker and dating, largely only comes with experience.

The seemingly "small" concerning behavior can, and often is, justified by ourselves and others if we don't know when we are being disrespected, or treated in a way that we aren't okay with. For example, he might take three days to return your phone call, always be running late, or changing plans at the last minute. This behavior could be rationalized; he could be busy at work, terrible with time management, indecisive, or he could be a psychopath who is toying with you.

The good news is we don't need to psychoanalyze him; you simply need to figure out if this kind of behavior is a problem. If it is, then it's time to determine if it's a deal-breaker. Or, are you willing to excuse a few occurrences but, if it keeps happening, then what? The decision is up to you.

Everybody has different deal-breakers, and they exist in all types of relationships. But, unfortunately, when it comes to romantic relationships, many people have limited their deal-breakers to two things: being cheated on or physically abused. And they view everything else as workable. This is a problem, as many other situations also warrant being deal-breakers.

The purpose of dating is to see how much compatibility is present across all of the essential areas: character, communication, commitment, life direction, having or not having children, handling finances, religious beliefs, just to name a few. If compatibility in any of these areas is missing, then there is no sense in staying in the relationship and working to improve it. The reason being is that doing so would require someone to make a massive compromise (that, even if made, has the potential for resentment in the future). These types of differences are profound, and requiring change is neither realistic nor fair, and will only lead to irritation, frustration, and wasted time for both people involved.

The fact is that anything can be a deal-breaker. This doesn't make you petty or difficult; it means you know what you will and won't compromise on. For example, some people don't want to date someone who works 70 hours a week, and some don't want to date someone who works 20 hours a week. Some don't want to date someone who has a few drinks every night, and others don't want to date someone who *doesn't* have a few drinks every night. For some, if a person has children, that's a deal-breaker, likewise if the other person does or doesn't want children. One person may want somebody who goes to church every week, whereas another person wants someone who only goes to church on the holidays, or is an atheist. The list is endless.

However, while a lot of deal-breakers are an individual decision based on what you are looking for in life, I believe some behaviors should be deal-breakers for everybody. Most deal-breaker behavior falls into what I consider to be the four horsemen of the relationship apocalypse: abuse, addiction, adultery, (bad) attitude. If any of these behaviors are present, the relationship is unbalanced and will, more than likely, topple over with time.

For example, there are no genuine workable solutions for being treated with a lack of dignity or respect, such as being yelled at, put down, patronized, treated with disdain, contempt, or hostility, lied to, exploited, you name it. It's okay for a person to get frustrated or angry, but it's not okay for them to become belittling or intimidating. If they were to talk to you in a way that you didn't like, how would they handle you asserting yourself? Do they become defensive, deflect from their behavior, or begin blaming or shaming you? If so, then they aren't being accountable, so expect this type of behavior to continue because they don't have any motivation to change.

If someone is disrespectful—especially if they are unapologetic and lack accountability for their behavior—then you can bet you will see that behavior again.

When it comes to workable behavior, three things are needed: 1. Knowing when you are experiencing behavior that you aren't okay with. 2. The ability to be assertive with the other person about your concerns. 3. Getting clear with yourself and with them on what will happen if their behavior doesn't change.

If you aren't certain that their behavior falls into deal-breaker territory, you can always approach it as though it's potentially workable and see what happens. After all, if you go through those three steps of workable behavior, and there is no lasting change, you won't be hanging on forever to try and make things work. You'll have a clear idea that it's time for you to leave.

Chapter 18: How can I tell if my standards are too high?

Dear Dana,

I've gone on several dates with several different men over the past six months and have stopped seeing each of them for various reasons. My friends say that my standards are too high, and I'm starting to worry that maybe they are right. How can I tell if my standards are too high?

~Sharon

Dear Sharon,

Let's start by examining the difference between high standards and healthy standards. To me, the word "healthy" is synonymous with "functional" or "working properly." Whereas "high standards" are equivalent to a level of perfection that is mainly unachievable or maintainable, and may not have anything to do with healthy standards.

Here's an example between how I see a high standard and a healthy standard: a high standard would be that you only date men who make more than $200,000 a year, whereas a healthy standard is that you only date men who are financially responsible and self-sufficient. The high standard, while seemingly specific, is actually vague as it doesn't have a basis in functional behavior. After all, a person can make a solid six-figures a year and be irresponsible with their money.

Healthy standards, in general, require that the other person be able to function as an adult. At a minimum, this would mean that they have solid character and effective communication. Some examples of healthy standards are: having manners, maintaining adult responsibilities, taking care of their physical and emotional health, being accountable for their behavior, and treating you and others with dignity, respect, and value, to name a few. You will have additional ones surrounding personal preference, such as children, religion, etc. In my opinion, these are healthy and reasonable standards. If a person is unable to function as an adult, it's not realistic to expect them to have a functional adult relationship. Anything less, and the dynamic is imbalanced, causing resentment, frustration, and anger to grow, more than likely leading to the relationship ending in the future.

An unhealthy standard would be a standard that isn't working well for you or the relationship. Expecting your partner to read your mind because you don't think you should have to communicate any issue you may have with them would be an unhealthy standard in a relationship. Victims of abuse are often on the receiving end of trying to live up to unhealthy standards of others. In order to keep a relationship going, they often unintentionally end up with low (or non-existent) standards for how they are treated. The thinking that drives this is that some crumbs of a relationship are better than nothing, but as the saying goes, "crumbs don't keep a person fed, they keep them starving." This is why it's so vital for survivors to be clear with themselves on the standards they expect from others for how they are to be treated.

I see a lot of people justifying a clear lack of respect, especially when it comes to dating. When someone is genuinely interested in a long-term relationship, they put in extra effort and treat you with respect as they are trying to prove themselves worthy of a place in your life. If a man is texting you at all hours of the day and night, or moves from mild flirting to sexual requests, or suggests you meet him at his house for the first date, these are all signs that he is not making any effort to make a good impression or looking to build a relationship.

Could this kind of low-effort behavior lead to a relationship? Sure, but realize that people don't tend to value what comes easy.

Additionally, it's worth keeping in mind that there are multiple definitions for what is meant by a functional relationship. For some, a functional relationship is one that is still going— even if that relationship is draining and damaging. As long as the relationship remains intact, they consider that a success. This mindset often comes from the idea that being alone is a problem. Perhaps they are intimidated by or fear the idea of being alone, or perhaps they think they are supposed to have a partner for whatever societal reasons. For some, this pressure to be in a relationship can be so great that being single feels like a failing on their part, a signal to the world that they are unlovable. Whereas others only want to date someone who will enhance their life. A person dating from a place of comfort and confidence isn't in a scramble to find someone so that they, or their lives, feel whole. Because the mindsets surrounding dating can be different, don't forget to consider this when weighing whatever advice you get.

After abuse, it's common for a person to have a low tolerance for any behavior that even comes close to what they experienced before and, as a result, to be quick in cutting off contact with anybody who exhibits such behavior. This is healthy if the behavior falls within deal-breaker territory; however, a skill many survivors struggle with is learning how to be self-protective through being assertive. An abuse survivor, at first, often goes back and forth between having overly flexible and overly rigid standards. They can feel afraid of being hurt again. At the same time, they may worry that their standards are too high and that they are pushing away potentially good people, even if those people continually cross their boundaries. But there is a middle ground here. We don't have to second-guess ourselves, wondering if we are making a big deal out of nothing. If we click with a person, but a boundary is crossed, or something concerns us, we can speak up and let them know, then see how they respond. Depending on this, we set the standard for how we are to be treated and if we should move forward. It doesn't matter whether or not your friends consider this a "high standard", what matters is that it is a healthy standard for you.

Chapter 19: How do I stop comparing this relationship to my previous one?

Dear Dana,

I have been dating Michael for about two years now. Before I was dating Michael, I was dating a man I'll call Carlos. Carlos was wonderful to me, and pretty much my best friend. I would have married Carlos had he not been killed in an accident. I'm sure there will always be a part of me that will miss and love him, but I thought I'd worked through a lot of my grief, as I was in counseling for about a year after he died. I started dating Michael about eighteen months later.

At first, things were great between us, but after we moved in together, he just didn't put any effort into our relationship or seem to care about how I felt. For example, he goes out with his friends several times a week to the bar, but then whenever I mention that I'd like to go to the movies with him, he says he doesn't have money. And even though he makes twice as much as I do, I pay for almost everything. He also goes out with female friends with whom I know he's had sex with in the recent past, and he gets upset with me if I tell him I'm not comfortable with this. Whenever I bring anything up to him, he accuses me of comparing him to Carlos, and I'm scared that he's right. How can I stop doing this and be more invested in my current relationship?

~ Maya

Dear Maya,

The comparison you are making between these two men doesn't seem to be because you have unresolved grief from the sudden death of Carlos. Sometimes when we find ourselves comparing one person or situation to another, it's because deep down, we know something isn't right, but we are struggling to consciously acknowledge it. Carlos sounds as though he was kind, considerate, compassionate, and made your relationship a priority, whereas Michael is behaving quite differently.

Outside of how Michael treats you, my concern is that you seem focused on keeping this relationship together— regardless of how much it costs you emotionally and financially— with the hopes that someday Michael will understand how hurtful his behavior is. Or he'll see how much you do for him so that he'll start appreciating, and treating, you in the same way that Carlos did. Trying to have a relationship with someone who isn't emotionally invested, and who is instead using their partner for sex, money, and a place to live is draining on every level.

Your frustration with Michael sounds like it's coming from repeatedly experiencing the same types of hurtful behavior from him, wondering why he won't change and act like he's in a relationship. Instead, I think you need to acknowledge the hard truth that a relationship with him is a one-way street where you give time, money, and multiple chances, and he continues doing whatever he wants regardless of how this makes you feel. That he dismisses your feelings and spins things around to where he claims you have the issue (your comparing him to Carlos), is a level of invalidation that would make anyone angry.

Frustration and anger happen when our expectations don't match reality. Your expectations of Michael's behavior don't match his behavior; that's why you are continually shocked and upset by it. If you allowed yourself to see his actions clearly, you would acknowledge that he is disrespectful. Unfortunately, so many of us stay, trying to prove our worth to people like this, thinking that if we can just get through to them that what they are doing is hurtful, they will start treating us better. We believe that if we can only communicate our needs more effectively, things will improve. This is wishful thinking on our end, and can keep us stuck in dynamics like this until things get so bad we are forced to leave. (Or until they leave us because they weren't that invested in the relationship to begin with.)

The issue here isn't that you are comparing Michael to Carlos and are, therefore, not invested enough in this relationship. The issue is that Michael has demonstrated that he is not invested in his relationship with you. Trying to make this dynamic work is an exercise in frustration because you can't fix Michael, or this relationship.

Take a moment and think about how you felt when you were dating Carlos. Odds are you felt safe, secure, important, valued, and loved. If you felt this way, then you probably also felt calm, relaxed, and comfortable around him. Now think about how you feel around Michael. Odds are you feel distrusting, insecure, unimportant, disregarded, and taken for granted. When a person feels this way, they also tend to feel anxious and depressed. A healthy relationship nourishes you. An unhealthy relationship is draining and feels toxic. Your concerns about Michael's behavior are valid. The next step is to take all the energy you are spending trying to get the relationship to work, and instead figure out where your deal-breakers are with his behavior, so you can know when it's time to move on.

Not every relationship is fixable, and sometimes the healthiest thing a person can do is to leave.

Chapter 20: Is name-calling a sign he will be abusive in the future?

Dear Dana,

I've been dating Tim for about eight months. I broke up with him a month ago because of his jealousy. My ex-husband was a jealous man, and I refuse to put up with that again. Tim apologized, and I took him back only to have his jealousy resurface because a man looked at me while we were out shopping together. However, this time he called me some pretty harsh names. Is being called names a red flag that he will be abusive in the future?

~ Rebecca

Dear Rebecca,

Yes, his jealousy, need for control, name-calling, and disrespect for your feelings are all major red flags worthy of being deal-breakers. As far as if he will be abusive in the future, please know that *what you are experiencing with him now is abuse,* and will more than likely get worse and/or become more frequent with time. For some, calling another person names may seem on the mild end of the abuse spectrum, but it's a huge red flag and perhaps the most significant indicator that more abuse will follow. The reason I say this is because it takes a lot of entitlement, a lack of self-control, and a lack of respect for the other person to call someone names. Not to mention he blamed and berated you for something you had no control over.

This incident shows that he has a skewed, and potentially dangerous, mindset when it comes to accountability, responsibility, and appropriate communication. Add jealousy to the mix, along with his lack of respect for your feelings or boundaries, and you have the makings for more abusive behavior to come. You've only seen the tip of the iceberg. We all get upset, but those who have appropriate boundaries know where the line is, and to not cross it, as hurtful things can't be unsaid.

A healthy relationship is one based on treating each other with respect, each partner cultivating a substantial amount of trust, the ability to work as a team, and for both people to have open, honest, sincere, and solution-oriented communication. You saw that his jealousy didn't fit within those criteria, and now you see more problematic behavior, so take some time and see where that fits into your idea of what a healthy relationship is. Consider taking a break from dating. Spend some time examining your standards for how you expect to be treated in a relationship, as you've already been down this road once with your ex-husband.

When people are involved in more than one abusive relationship, there is often (but not always) disempowering messages occurring at a subconscious level. For example, they might be misinterpreting problematic behavior, such as someone being controlling or jealous for that person being concerned or caring. Or, if they have experienced worse forms of abuse in the past, they may think what they are experiencing now isn't that bad, and is therefore workable. Or, they may be getting well-intended bad advice (such as, "if he's that jealous he must really like you") that is contributing to their confusion. Or, they have feelings for the person, are tired of dating, afraid of starting over, or think this is as good as things get, and so are trying to convince themselves that being disrespected is no big deal.

When we misread or minimize problematic behavior, it's usually because we want to keep the relationship going and, deep down, we don't feel like we deserve better. We think it's okay to settle for crumbs of attention, affection, kindness, or loyalty, perhaps reasoning that no one is perfect, so we shouldn't have standards that are too high. Or maybe we think that crumbs are better than nothing. If you do decide to stay, I strongly encourage you to become clear on what specific behaviors you need to see change and in what time frame (bearing in mind that some behavior changes, as you experienced, are temporary). This way, you will have the clarity you need to move on.

.Chapter 21: Is it common to be in more than one abusive relationship?

Dear Dana,

Is it common to be abused more than once? My ex was physically and sexually abusive. After we divorced, I didn't date anyone for close to five years and took that time to heal. I swore to myself that I'd never date anyone like that again, but my new boyfriend turned out to be verbally and emotionally abusive. He said things that hurt more than any of the physical abuse I had experienced in the other relationship.

Sometimes I blame myself, as I should have seen the signs because I had already been through it. At the same time, the abuse was so different; it was two unique experiences. What is wrong with me that I stayed with two abusive men? I guess I need to get better at learning some of the red flags. I suppose I just tend to think that other people are inherently good, and so when they aren't, I make excuses for their behavior.

~ Kristen

Dear Kristen,

Unfortunately, yes, it is common for survivors of abuse to experience several abusive partners. The reason is that there are lots of unconscious patterns and dysfunctional messages at work. Additionally, as you mentioned, every abusive person, and every abusive relationship, can be very different. Because of this, the solution doesn't involve getting better with identifying red flags; it's about becoming more in tune with three things: identifying when you are being treated in a way that makes you uncomfortable; knowing how to handle an uncomfortable situation when it happens; and understanding when it's time to end a relationship.

If you are inclined to believe that everyone is good and has good intentions, then this is a problem, because the world is full of all kinds of people—many of whom don't have good intentions. There are many good, decent people out there. However, we have to be able to discern good behavior from bad behavior. If we are glossing over the bad, making excuses for it, then we aren't just looking for the good in others, we are unknowingly justifying our mistreatment.

The reality is it doesn't matter why someone does what they do. It doesn't matter if they had a bad childhood, a bad day, or are in a bad mood. The expectation is that people, especially adults, can moderate their behavior and treat others respectfully regardless of how they feel. Think about it this way: this is the expectation we have from a work environment, right? We expect our co-workers and even our boss to treat us and others with respect and dignity at all times regardless of whether or not they're upset. Those who throw a fit because something doesn't go their way, or because they are in a bad mood, get fired, or those around them start quitting.

If you are continually minimizing hurtful behavior and your resulting uneasiness, then you aren't seeing or responding to reality. You are living in a hope-fueled fantasy. We all do this to some degree, especially when we are trying to get our needs met. After all, it can be difficult to accept a painful reality when we have an emotional (or in the case of a job, financial) investment in staying. Denial is more than just refusing to see things as they are, denial is also delusion—believing things can be how we want them to be when that is highly unlikely.

The reason I mentioned that it won't help to focus more identifying red flags is because doing so will only serve to make you anxious and continually second guess yourself. I understand how red flags can be helpful, but knowing specific red flags is only useful if those same behaviors present themselves in the same way next time. Unfortunately, as you've experienced, this isn't always the case. This is why identifying when you feel uncomfortable, and responding in a way that honors your feelings, is everything.

For example, several years ago, there were scams on Craigslist where people were listing cars for sale that were several thousand dollars less than what a vehicle like that would typically cost. The poster also added that the reason for this was because they were in the military, being deployed overseas soon, and needed to sell the car. This was a scam, and Craigslist finally put a big warning on the "For Sale" section of their site saying something along the lines that 100% of ads offering to ship cars were scams and not to wire anyone money. So knowing that specific type of scam was helpful, but it won't keep a person 100% safe as manipulators always switch up their game when the game stops working. There are lots of scams out there, from relationship scams, housing scams, phone calls saying they are from the IRS and that we owe money, pretending to be a family member in trouble, and so on. Learning the red flags and trying to follow them exactly won't help as each scam and scammer is different. A good start is to be honest with yourself if something feels "off." At that point, you can seek verification (such as calling the IRS directly), putting a deposit on a credit card (because charges can be disputed), and not "loaning" money you can't afford to lose. These actions are not being paranoid, they are part of being self-protective.

When you are dating, it's essential to use that same degree of self-protection by utilizing your boundaries, standards, and deal-breakers. The less you tolerate being disrespected, the quicker you will walk away from relationships if this kind of behavior surfaces.

Hopefully, you now feel more validated in that there is no

excuse for abuse, and that you didn't cause it or deserve it. Abuse of all kinds can be tricky to identify, and abusers can make you feel as though you are the one with the problem because, in their minds, their mistreatment is justified. If you forget to turn the heat down before you left for work, they may feel entitled to rage at you when you get home. If you ask them about the woman who keeps texting them at night, they may feel justified in berating, belittling, or becoming physical with you—accusing you of starting a fight, or being jealous and controlling.

It can be easy for a person to get knocked off-center and believe that they are somehow at fault for being abused, so much so that they might not even recognize their partner's behavior as abuse. They may think they are being treated appropriately in light of whatever "wrong" they had done. This leads the target of abuse to doubling or tripling up their efforts not to upset their partner, but that never works, as that's not the problem. The problem is that their partner feels entitled to disrespect others and steamroll over their boundaries. It's important to know what you will and won't tolerate in a relationship, so you don't spend years, or decades, being verbally or otherwise abused. No one should have to earn, argue, or fight for dignity and respect. These are the basics of appropriate behavior towards others, especially in a relationship.

Chapter 22: How do I know if I'm moving too slow?

Dear Dana,

You say I need to set the pace, but I'm afraid of going too slow and my boyfriend losing interest and leaving. How do I know if I'm going too slow?

~ Andrea

Dear Andrea,

I encourage people to move at the pace in which they are most comfortable because they will not only have greater peace of mind but, in doing so, they also aren't allowing the other person to dictate how fast things move. Many, if not most, manipulative people want what they want when they want it, and will do what they can to push others into giving in to them. Moving faster may keep the other person around, but for how long and at what cost to your inner peace? If the result of the other person staying around is that you feel anxious, unhinged, uncomfortable, and as though you are acting in ways that make you uncomfortable, then the relationship isn't worth it, because nothing is worth feeling this way. And if you are thinking that a relationship is worth you feeling this uneasy, then it's worth exploring why you are valuing a relationship more than your peace of mind.

Everyone moves at a different pace. Some people have sex on the first date, some have sex around the third date, some have sex several months in, and some wait to have sex until marriage. Will your pace, just like the rest of your boundaries or standards, run some people off? Yes, absolutely—but that's a good thing! If your standards and boundaries didn't turn some people off, then there's a problem. Your life will start to work, and you will find people that fit what you are looking for, when you get out of this fear-driven mindset that, by having standards and boundaries, you will scare off everyone. You won't. Your boundaries will only scare off the people that aren't right for you.

Since everyone's pace is different, it's crucial to know what is comfortable for you. Try to avoid comparing your pace to someone else's, or seeking validation from other people for the speed at which you need to move. If you are still not sure whether or not you are moving at a good pace, take some time to examine how you feel. If you leave a date feeling like you've revealed too much, talked too much, or had sex too soon, then you've moved faster than what is right for you.

Ask yourself: if you were to have sex with this person or tell them deeply personal things about yourself, how would you feel about that in the morning? If you'd be fearful they wouldn't call again, or you are unsure of how they will handle what you've told them, then the relationship hasn't gone through enough to be stable, and it's unclear if this person is emotionally safe or not. You can determine a good pace by the different mile markers you've reached. How has this person responded to things you've told them? How do they handle being frustrated, upset, or not getting their way? How do they respond when you disagree with them or set a boundary? Have you both spoken up about what your expectations are for a relationship, and what each of you is looking for in another person?

The answers to these questions will help you to determine the pace in which you move. Remember, the right pace is the one in which you are most comfortable. If you lose anybody because you aren't moving fast enough, then they weren't the right person for you.

Chapter 23: How do I stop attracting narcissists?

Dear Dana,

I swear, I'm starting to feel like a magnet for narcissists! The last five people I've had in my life, either as friends or men I've gone on dates with, seemed great. But over the next few weeks or months, they turned out to be self-absorbed, controlling, possessive, demanding, exhausting, and overall lacking in accountability for their behavior. I'm so sick of dealing with people like this. How on earth do I stop attracting narcissists?

~ Joanna

Dear Joanna,

You are asking one of my absolute favorite questions. I love this question so much because I've found it to be one that has the potential to radically change a person's mindset and worldview when it comes to how they interact with others.

This question is such a game-changer because *the answer to it involves seeing where you are placing your control.* The question of "How do I stop attracting narcissists?" shows a mindset of someone who wants to have control in their life, but still feels helpless. I say this is because the first part of the question shows accountability and ownership by asking, "How do I…" however, the question ends with, "stop attracting narcissists?"

We all attract a wide range of people, and we can't control who we attract, so focusing on changing something we can't control will only lead to confusion, frustration, or feelings of hopelessness. Think of it this way, if someone asked how they could stop attracting people who have a problem with gambling or alcohol, advising them to avoid casinos or bars only helps to a point. A person could still meet a gambler or alcoholic at work, church, volunteering, you name it. If they have a pattern of dating or befriending the same types of people, they would be better off asking themselves, "What is it about these people that I find so attractive?" Or, "How can I get problematic people out of my life sooner?" When a person owns their power (otherwise known as having an internal locus of control), they are in the driver's seat. It is also essential to know that all problematic people come across differently. For example, some are romantic and charming, and others are insufferable and selfish. So don't stress if a manipulator flies under your radar for a bit. Because there is such a wide range of ways a problematic person can come across, the only way we can tell if somebody is deeply dysfunctional (outside of obviously concerning behavior), is to do what we need to be doing with everyone in our life: observe how they treat us and others, and how they respond to our boundaries.

Now, you may be thinking that attracting predatory people is different. You may have heard that predatory people can walk into a room and know who to target. There is some truth to this—but only if they are looking for someone vulnerable. Predatory people are not utilizing some sort of extra-sensory ability when selecting an easy target. Easy targets tend to be those who are young and naive, older and gullible, lonely, relatively isolated, or lacking a support system. These people may feel scared, hurt, insecure, overwhelmed, or thirsty for attention and validation. Some of these things we can do something about and others we can't. Staying safe isn't about eliminating all of our vulnerabilities, as that's impossible. We will always have weaknesses, that's part of being human.

What's important is that we are aware of our vulnerabilities so they aren't easily exploited. And we can do as much as possible to live a full life we enjoy so that we aren't starved out for attention, affection, or fun and looking towards someone else to fill that need for us.

So, while wolves will target the sheep that are either on the fringes or away from the pack, if there is more than one sheep that meets these criteria, the wolf will then be drawn to the sheep that has a limp, or some kind of injury making it unable to run fast. Although this approach is used some of the time it is not, exclusively, how predators operate. Other times the flock might not have any stragglers, young, old, or injured sheep. When this is the case, a wolf is merely going to pick one and go after it.

So, while exploitative people may go after low-hanging fruit, many abusers don't have a hidden agenda or even understand that their behavior is a problem. They just believe they are entitled to lash out at others if they feel like it, and they get offended if we try to set boundaries with them because they don't respect boundaries. These types of abusive people who are less aware of the inappropriateness of their actions, may simply be attracted to someone in a sincere, ordinary way, not because they have necessarily targeted that person. However, other kinds of abusers are more attracted to what a person has to offer them, such as social status, a place to stay, money, you name it.

Gold-diggers, or scammers of any kind, would be an example of this type of behavior. They are simply after money. If a person has a significant amount of money, odds are they will attract gold-diggers. Even if they live modestly, sometimes word gets out, and false friends will surface. There is nothing a person can do to prevent these kinds of people from being attracted to them. All they can do is be cautious and hold their boundaries if anybody attempts to take advantage of them.

The only way to repel exploitative people is to go slow, maintain healthy boundaries, and avoid over-giving. Once a problematic person realizes that you won't tolerate being mistreated or used as a doormat, they will move on. Some, however, will try to guilt or persuade you into giving them another chance. They may tell you everything you want to hear or blame you for their issues. Having deal-breakers is vital so you don't spend unnecessary time hanging on to a relationship that isn't there. Manipulative and abusive people tend to go back to those who tolerate mistreatment and those who, they know, with time and pressure, will wear down and give in to them.

So remember, while we can't control who is attracted to us, and we may or may not spot problematic behavior during the first few weeks of getting to know someone, we can control our boundaries and how long we keep someone in our lives.

Chapter 24: What is a dysfunctional relationship?

Dear Dana,

I hear the term "dysfunctional relationship" used a lot, and I'm embarrassed to say that I'm not exactly sure what it means. I asked a friend of mine, and she laughed, saying that all relationships are somewhat dysfunctional. Is this true, and if not, what makes a relationship dysfunctional?

~ Emily

Dear Emily,

You are right in that the term "dysfunctional relationship" is used quite a bit. While dysfunction can be present to some degree in all relationships, perhaps the bigger question is, when is it a problem? Dysfunction, like most everything else in life, exists on a spectrum ranging from mild to major. Because the term "dysfunctional relationship" is so over-used, the real meaning becomes diluted with common jokes like "we put the fun in dysfunctional." Or, over-use can have the opposite effect. A term such as "dysfunctional relationship" can feel so heavy and exclusive to those relationships in which extreme addiction or abuse is present. We might find ourselves hesitant to label any relationship this way, concerned about making a big deal out of "nothing" because somewhere, someone has it worse.

For these reasons, I think it can help to back up a bit and look at the definition of the word "dysfunctional." When something is dysfunctional, it is not functioning, or not working as it should. A dysfunctional relationship then is one that isn't working. As with anything else, the range of something not working falls on a spectrum ranging from mild to major. I find it helpful to think of the functionality of relationships like the functionality of cars. There is a wide variety of ways a car could become non-functional from having a flat tire to missing an engine. It doesn't matter if the issue is mild or major, as the result is the same: the car is un-drivable. Additionally, the issues other people have with their own cars doesn't make our car's issue any better or worse.

All relationships have their moments when disagreements surface, feelings are hurt, and boundaries are crossed. What makes a relationship dysfunctional is how one or more people in that relationship go about handling conflict, stress, confrontation, or issues in general. Dysfunctional communication doesn't work in the long run, it only serves to create more significant issues as time goes on. Dysfunctional families handle issues in a combination of passive, passive-aggressive, or aggressive ways.

Some examples of passive behavior would be avoidance or people-pleasing.

Some examples of passive-aggressive behavior would be the silent treatment, withholding vital information, planting seeds of jealousy or hostility, and icy looks or behavior.

Some examples of aggressive behavior would be cussing, yelling, hitting, or threatening.

In short, issues are handled in every way except through assertive behavior. Boundaries are blurred or non-existent, and being a part of the family may require members to sacrifice large parts of who they are. A dysfunctional family is a perpetually frustrating and crazy-making family—usually, one that relies heavily on members treading lightly around, or outright avoiding specific topics.

These types of dynamics are exhausting as there is so much energy devoted to bypassing the real issues at hand. Each time conflict or confrontation surfaces, it is denied, minimized, justified, or dismissed by blaming another person. Problems are rarely resolved, and instead, family members cope as best as they can. Unfortunately, many cope in ways that provide immediate relief, but have negative consequences in the long term. A breakdown of communication, inappropriate expectations, and blurred boundaries are primary reasons why addictions are so common in dysfunctional families.

You can tell how functional or dysfunctional a relationship is for you based in large part by how you feel. If you find yourself rehashing conversations, feeling continually anxious, upset, frustrated, invalidated, ignored, or fearful, these are all signs that this relationship is out-of-balance, dysfunctional, and not working for you. The key here is that we can't look to others to become functional for the relationship to become balanced. *You can only balance your boundaries, even if (especially if) it's the other people in your life that are the ones with the major issues.* You only have control over yourself. Maintaining your boundaries around others is the only way to limit the negative impact of dysfunctional behavior.

Maintaining boundaries is essential to an individual's healthy functionality. Without boundaries, there is dysfunction, and the person suffers. Those who grew up in homes where functional boundaries, expectations, standards, or behaviors weren't the norm may have never realized they had a right to be selective or protective when it came to their relationships with others. The result is the over-reliance on others to determine where our boundaries are (even when we don't). If we feel disrespected, the only action possible is to hold onto hope that the mistreatment will stop. It often takes decades of abuse before a person realizes this mistreatment is not okay, and they can assert themselves by either minimizing, or completely cutting off, contact with the offending person.

A lesson that is all too often hard-won (and difficult to accept as it can feel like victim-blaming) is that the inability to maintain functional boundaries is a form of unconscious self-harm that is the result of dysfunctional messages received from others—usually starting in childhood. Unfortunately, for many, healthy boundaries weren't allowed, taught, or role modeled. Instead, the messages received were that anger wasn't justified or appropriate, forgiveness in the form of continual allowance of hurtful behavior was expected and the right thing to do, saying no was rude and not working as a team, and that family is forever no matter how horribly they behave.

Blurred or non-existent boundaries lead to long-term consequences such as poor health, anxiety, depression, addiction, and so on. Once you connect to your inherent value as a person, you will find it easier to assert your boundaries and effectively handle problematic people and situations. Establishing boundaries can be awkward and uncomfortable, but boundaries are essential to having manageable or functional relationships in your life. Limiting the dysfunction in your life will result in more peace. Again, this is not to say that doing so will be easy.

Establishing boundaries in an already dysfunctional environment (like a family or workplace) is significantly more challenging than setting boundaries with someone with whom you choose to start a balanced relationship. However, it is important to note that having firm boundaries with difficult people will make the relationship tolerable, but it won't make it healthy or functional. For a relationship to be nourishing, both people need healthy boundaries and the ability to communicate effectively when those boundaries are crossed.

Chapter 25: How can I recognize when I'm talking to an abusive person?

Dear Dana,

I have had the worst luck with online dating. Every man I've gone out with has ended up being verbally and emotionally abusive. How do I recognize when I am talking to an abuser before I agree to meet?

~ Amanda

Dear Amanda,

Not all people with abusive behavior are the same, and some can hide their behavior better and for longer than others. Because of this, you might not be able to tell a whole lot about somebody before you meet them in person. However, there are overt signs, which include: calling you pet names right away, texting or calling you at all hours, speaking disrespectfully and harshly about others, asking for sexy pictures of you, pressuring you to do things you aren't comfortable doing or not taking "no" for an answer. Any of these are not the actions of a person who respects you.

When you are texting or speaking on the phone with someone, pay attention to how they respond to you having a differing opinion, disagreeing with them, or saying "no." Do they tease you, use sarcasm, or joke in a way that doesn't sit well with you? For example, let's say that they invite you to a bar for a drink, but you suggest a coffee shop, and they 'playfully' or 'sweetly' call you a "Goody-two-shoes." You might not see it as being disrespectful or pushing your boundaries, but it is, and it's this kind of more subtle behavior that gets brushed off by someone thinking that they are too sensitive. On the more obvious end of the spectrum, do they become loud, intimidating, belittling, shaming, blaming, disrespectful, or do they shut down all communication? If so, don't waste your time meeting them because these are all signs of significant emotional immaturity, and are forms of verbal and emotional abuse that, you can be sure, you'll see a lot more of in the future.

The timing of this bad behavior is also crucial because most people (including abusive people) can hold it together and be on their best behavior during this initial phase when both people are trying to make a good impression. If a person can't be on their best behavior even during this time, then it's a massive problem because, once they settle in, their behavior will be significantly worse. It's like if a person is in a job interview and they become belligerent, intimidating, loud, or inappropriate, there's no need to call this person back for a second interview as you've seen enough to tell that their behavior is going to be a nightmare. There are many other candidates out there; there's no need to hire someone who has already shown you they are going to be fired, or someone you wish you could fire soon.

So, while there are no guaranteed ways to identify an abuser before agreeing to meet, knowing when you are being treated in an uncomfortable way, and how to handle that, goes a long way towards keeping yourself safe.

Chapter 26: Are there questions I can ask to determine if a person is a narcissist?

Dear Dana,

I came across an article the other day that mentioned there were some questions a person could ask to determine whether someone was a narcissist. Is this true? If so, what questions should I be asking?

~ Laura

Dear Laura,

I always cringe when someone mentions that they heard about some shortcuts to determine if someone is a narcissist. While I can understand the appeal of wanting to know some simple way to keep energy vampires out of your life, please know that articles and videos like this are more damaging than helpful. Because this question is so frequently asked, let's examine it. I've heard people recommend: directly asking someone if they are a narcissist, asking them what they learned from their last relationship, or paying attention to how they treat the waiter.

While some narcissistic and problematic people will reveal themselves in this way, those with a reasonable degree of emotional intelligence know how to avoid being detected by these types of methods.

So these questions will only help you to spot the more obviously problematic people out there and are nowhere near 100% accurate. These types of questions are equivalent to trying to figure out if someone is a serial killer, thief, or child molester by merely asking them directly.

There are no questions you can ask someone that can guarantee if they are or aren't a narcissist. If anything, these questions provide a false sense of security and can be very misleading. I remember some talk show covered this topic and said one of the indicators was how they treat the waiter, and that being rude to the waiter is a big red flag. While I agree with this, there are also lots of abusive people who are incredibly charming and who treat waiters fabulously. For many survivors, hearing about such cut-and-dry red flags as this would only serve to fuel their confusion about their partner. Instead of trying to determine whether or not their partner is a narcissist (or sociopath/psychopath) survivors would do better to focus on problematic behavior.

The reality is that narcissists exist on a continuum ranging from annoying to deadly, and obvious to subtle. Keep in mind that a person doesn't need to be a narcissist to be problematic, and a person doesn't need to be abusive for you not to want to spend time with them. This is your life, and you determine what is and isn't acceptable to have within it and to what degree. After all, you have to live with the results of your decisions, not me, your therapist, friends, or family. For these reasons, you are better off switching your focus from trying to identify who is and isn't a narcissist, to turning inward and identifying what behavior is and isn't okay with you.

The most accurate way to tell if a person is problematic is to observe their behavior as well as to notice how you feel around them. How do they treat you and others? Mainly, how do they treat your boundaries and the boundaries of others? Do you feel drained of energy, uncomfortable, icky, irritated, annoyed, defensive, anxious, or on-guard? If so, these are signs that you don't feel safe with this person (emotionally, and maybe even physically) and that distancing yourself from them might be a good idea. Remember, being uncomfortable around someone is reason enough not to want to see them again. You don't need to wait until someone's behavior escalates to the point where you have certainty that they are a creep, predator, or dangerous, to walk away.

Chapter 27: Am I jealous and controlling?

Dear Dana,

My boyfriend is good friends with his ex-girlfriend, and I am not okay with this. I'm not usually a jealous person, but since they share a past, I'm not comfortable with how much time they now spend together. I've brought up my concerns with him, and he gets upset. He's told me numerous times his friendship with her is "nothing" and accuses me of being jealous and trying to control him. Am I unreasonable for having an issue with him spending time with his ex?

~ Pauline

Dear Pauline,

It is entirely reasonable to have a problem with your boyfriend spending time with his ex. After all, his ex is someone with whom he had an intimate relationship, and it can be very easy for that door to be reopened. Additionally, when exes are friends, there is a strong chance that at least one of them still has feelings for the other. Even if there are no romantic feelings involved in the friendship, a partner's primary focus, in terms of relationships, should be on the one they are currently in. For him to have a relationship with his ex or any other woman, these potential issues need to be discussed and resolved. Emotional safety is vital in a relationship. This means both of you listen when you each express yourselves. And, if there are hurt or insecure feelings, those feelings are addressed and resolved, not minimized and invalidated.

If his friendship with her means "nothing," then he shouldn't be willing to jeopardize his relationship with you over "nothing." If this doesn't concern him, then he doesn't place much value on your relationship. If there truly is nothing going on then, at minimum, it would be appropriate to include you whenever they spend time together. He should not be calling or messaging her at all hours, spending time with her when you aren't around, and then getting upset when you have a problem with this. That's ridiculous, and not the behavior of someone who values their partner or their relationship. What I come across a lot of is one partner cheating or leaving the door open to cheat with so-called "friends." They hide their phone, secretly spend time with people they are attracted to, and other kinds of dishonest, deceptive actions, and then accuse their partner of being jealous and controlling if their partner has an issue with their inappropriate behavior.

It's perfectly fine if you don't want to date a man who is still in regular communication with his ex. This is about knowing your limits. This doesn't mean you are jealous, uptight, insecure, or that your thinking is old-fashioned or outdated. It means that you don't want to date someone who still spends time with their former partners. Additionally, I think it's entirely reasonable to have an issue with your partner spending time with any members of the opposite sex, regardless of whether or not they've been sexually involved. And if you were a man and he was a woman, I'd tell him the same thing. Having opposite-sex friends, especially ones where sexual attraction was at one time involved is, more often than not, going to cause problems.

Chapter 28: Am I wrong for not wanting to be his friend?

Dear Dana,

I'd been dating this guy for five months, and I thought it was the best relationship ever. (It was my first relationship since things ended with my abusive ex.) But he disappeared on me for about two weeks, then resurfaced saying he wasn't ready for anything serious and just wanted to be friends. I was crushed. I'm pretty sure he's back with his ex-girlfriend, whom he swore was just a friend. I was so hurt and vowed never to talk to him again…until he reached out to me today. I tried to explain to him how hurt I was, and that I didn't think I could be friends with him. He became angry and told me I was immature. My friends tell me that maybe he needs time, and that since we got along so well, I should be reconnect with him and spend time with him as a friend…but I don't know if I could or should do that. I was wondering what you think. Am I immature for not wanting to be friends with him?

~ Andy

Dear Andy,

All relationships start with some sort of idealize phase where things are, well, ideal. This is the fantasy part of a relationship—it isn't real. Once both people start becoming more comfortable around each other, the more the fantasy ends, and the reality begins. The challenge with the idealize stage is that it feels so perfect and wonderful that, if we don't see it as a fantasy, we will forever chase this stage in hopes of getting it back.

The challenge with the idealize stage is that it feels so perfect, so wonderful that, if we don't see it as infatuation, we are forever chasing this stage in hopes of getting it back. So while the first five months were wonderful for you, I'm sorry to say that it doesn't sound like it meant that much to him if he was able to disappear, and only resurface because he said he wanted to be friends (which is often just code for keeping someone on the back burner). Friends don't treat each other like this.

Initially, there was this intense connection to him, whether that was intended on his part, I can't say, but it sounds like he wants to keep you around as a backup plan. I have to say that it's jaw-dropping for him to suggest being friends because, by my definition, a friend is someone you can rely on, and this guy's behavior has demonstrated that you can't depend on him. Friends respect your boundaries, they don't invalidate your feelings or spin things around to blame you, and if they want to be in a happy relationship with someone else, they don't turn their former lovers into friends and keep them waiting in the wings. What also concerns me is that he can go from having this seemingly incredible connection to "just friends" at the flip of a switch. It would be challenging to ever feel emotionally secure in a relationship with a person like this, as you'd forever be wondering if that switch might flip again.

Additionally, he knows if you decide to accept his "friendship," you will more than likely be holding onto hope and tripling up your efforts to bring him back into a relationship. If he is seeing someone else, then keep in mind that your presence as a "friend" is also there as a reminder for the other woman that he has options, making her anxious in the process.

In short, no, you are not immature by declining his "friendship." A friend is someone you can rely on, and this guy's behavior has shown that you can't depend on him. Not only that, but he doesn't respect your boundaries, he invalidates your feelings, and spins things around to blame you. If anything, I think you are being very mature and have a good grasp of your self-worth to pass on his offer. You want someone who sees your worth, who is interested and able to be in a committed relationship, and who is capable of treating you like an option, not a priority. Until then, you are wise to move on.

Chapter 29: How can I tell if I'm in an abusive relationship?

Dear Dana,

Things between my boyfriend and me haven't been good for a while. I've caught him cheating twice over the past four years, and a lot of my friends have quit talking to me because they don't like him. My mom told me the other day that she didn't like how he treated me, so I've started to wonder if I am in an abusive relationship. He's never hit me. I guess what I'm asking is, is there a way to tell if I'm in an abusive relationship?

~ Hannah

Dear Hannah,

I can certainly understand your confusion because when most people think of an abusive relationship, they think of extreme physical abuse that leaves bruises and broken bones. However, the truth is that many abusive relationships never get to that extreme, but they are just as damaging.

Most people think an abusive relationship is only abusive if there is physical abuse going on. The truth is that there are seven types of abuse: verbal, emotional, psychological, sexual, financial, physical, and spiritual. For a relationship to be abusive, one or more forms of abuse need to be present. Understanding what abusive behavior is can be confusing. Most people understand what physical and sexual abuse are because there are often visual signs that abuse has occurred. Emotional, verbal, and psychological abuse can be more difficult to pinpoint as it includes a wide range of behavior that doesn't leave concrete proof. At the core, all abusive behavior is the mistreatment of another, and violating their boundaries through hurtful behavior.

At the center of abusive behavior is the mindset of entitlement, and behavior with no understanding and/or respect for another's boundaries. The vast majority of the time, there is more than one type of abuse in a relationship or dynamic. Physical abuse is a "late-stage" of abuse that often starts with verbal and emotional abuse. Abusive behavior tends to get worse over time, not better. All forms of abuse are incredibly damaging, so please don't think that "just" because you aren't hit, doesn't mean that you aren't hurt.

Abusive relationships tend to start gradually with seemingly "small" boundary pushes, or "digs" are made about a person's appearance, gender, intelligence, profession, hopes, dreams, family, friends, or things that they are either proud of or sensitive about and grow with time.

Abusive behavior is a slow grinding down of the one being targeted. Perhaps the best way to describe it is to use the the parable of "how to boil a frog." The lesson goes that if you want to boil a frog, you have to place it in a pot of lukewarm water and slowly turn the heat up, this way the frog doesn't realize what's happening until it's too late--because if you were to throw a frog into boiling water, it would immediately jump out.

Abuse happens the same way.

And, because abusive relationships often start mildly, by the time things have really changed it can be challenging to see the full scope of the problem because, odds are, the victim has an emotional investment in the relationship. Also, abusive people are rarely abusive 100% of the time. They may "only" be abusive 5% of the time, or even 1% of the time. And, because they aren't abusive all the time, and because when things are good, they are really good, it can be hard to figure out when to stay and when to leave. And because they aren't abusive all the time, and because when things are good, they are often really good, it can be hard to figure out when to stay and when to leave.

For this reason, it can be helpful to instead look at abusive relationships as "toxic" or "poisonous." Looking at them in this way helps a person to better understand the severity of the situation. Relationships are like food. They are meant to be empowering and nourishing. We would never drink water, which was 5% or even 1% poisonous, so why be in a poisonous relationship?

The best way to tell if a relationship is abusive or toxic is to pay attention to how you feel. The mistake a lot of people make is to try and get clarity from their partner as to why their partner's behavior is so confusing. But, if your partner is manipulative or abusive in any way, you will not get clarity, only more manipulation and abuse. And, you may be told, any mistreatment on their part was somehow your fault. Overall, questioning whether or not you are in an abusive relationships is a red flag in and of itself.

Chapter 30: Is this an example of someone's mask slipping?

Dear Dana,

I feel like I'm still learning to spot red flags and set boundaries. After things ended with my abusive ex, I dated this other guy for five months. It was the best relationship ever, but then he sort of disappeared on me for a while, then broke up with me out of the blue and said he wanted to be just friends. I was close to never talking to him again until he reached out to me today. But when I tried to set a boundary, he would tell me I was uptight, trying to punish him, making a big deal out of nothing, or would shift the conversation to where he'd focus on everything I did that he didn't like. I can't believe I cried over this guy, uggghhh. He did have a way of saying jokes that rubbed me the wrong way, but I always wrote them off as a weird sense of humor and thought I was just being triggered due to my past experiences. I would never get back with him, but I was wondering what you think: is this an example of his mask slipping?

~ Angie

Dear Angie,

As far as the concept of someone's mask slipping, this refers to a radical shift in their behavior where a different side of them is seen. Although it sounds like his mask did slip somewhat when he went from being friendly, so that you'd let him come over, to being rude when you said no, it seems to me that this guy has a pattern of being a jerk. Let's review a bit. He "joked" around with you in ways that you didn't like. He disappeared on you, then broke up with you, then disrespected your boundaries.

It took you some time to see his lack of respect clearly, and that's okay because you eventually did see it, realizing this guy is no prize. Acknowledging this can be difficult, especially when things were great at first, and we want to believe that they can go back to being that way.

I've seen survivors of abuse time and again try to understand the behavior of others in a piece-by-piece kind of way, asking themselves (and others) questions such as, "Is this an example of his mask slipping?" "Is this love bombing?" "Is this person a narcissist?" Trying to figure out the behavior of others like this often leads to more confusion than clarity because you could ask ten people and get ten different answers. The kicker is that regardless of whether or not a person's behavior fits a definition, or even what others say—it doesn't matter. What matters is how you feel about how you are being treated. If someone is disrespecting you or treating you like an option instead of a priority, then this isn't a person who values you or having a relationship with you, and you would do best to move on.

Chapter 31: What traits attract abusive men?

Dear Dana,

My therapist told me two disturbing things at our last session. She said that abusive men know what character traits to look for and that they can instantly spot their next target. And then she told me that women who have been in more than one abusive relationship attract abusive men. This has been my pattern! I dated one man who was abusive and then after that relationship ended, I went out with two more men who seemed wonderful, but then turned out to be complete liars. I googled the last guy, and it turned out he had a history of assault and domestic violence.

What are these characteristics abusers look for, and how do I get rid of them? I am glad I am smart enough to run, but how do I get free of this target I seem to have on me?

~ Victoria

Dear Victoria,

Most of us have heard this advice, usually on some daytime talk show or news clip where violent criminals, child molesters, or a mental health professional talk about how predatory people can spot their next target. They often mention that those who seem kind, compassionate, alone, or seem lonely, walk with their head down, or appear meek are targeted, but this isn't always the case.

I've come across many mental health professionals who have, with the best of intentions, told their clients the same thing. However, this well-intended and somewhat alarming advice is incredibly damaging because survivors will spend large amounts of time examining various traits that might make them a target. They may start going to great lengths to change who they are to prevent being a target. They may make less or more conversation or eye contact, or they may dress more or less conservatively or more confidently—whatever they think might help to avoid being targeted. And if they continue to get targeted by abusive people, they may continue to erase more of themselves, thinking this is what they need to do to stay safe. The reality is that every abuser targets different people for different reasons.

Sure, many targets are those who seem like they'd be easy to pick off from the herd, but there are also many predators out there who like the thrill of the hunt and seek out those who are a challenge. Some predatory people don't even think of their behavior as problematic. When they do become verbally, emotionally, physically, or sexually abusive, they feel entitled to behave this way because, in their mind, the other person did something to deserve it.

The way I read your question is, "I'm glad I am smart enough to run, but I am so tired of running. Is there any way I can get rid of this target I seem to have on me, so I don't have to waste so much time dealing with, then running from, these problematic people?" Unfortunately, while it would be nice just to adopt some character trait or behavior that prevents these people from entering our lives in the first place, so we don't have to waste any time with them, that's not possible. We all attract a wide variety of people, and we have no control over who we attract. *What we can control is to what degree we let problematic people into our lives, and for how long.*

With that said, some personality and character traits are more frequently exploited than others. These traits, when balanced, are considered the foundation for appropriate behavior; they are what make someone polite, personable, and overall enjoyable to be around. However, if these traits are extreme, they can become a problem. Here is a rundown of some imbalanced traits:

- Commitment at all cost (no matter how much they are mistreated, abused, cheated on, lied to, etc.)

- Putting others first (at the expense of themselves)

- Unending second chances (when the problematic behavior keeps happening)

- Seeing and assuming the best in others (and glossing over bad behavior)

- Compassion and rationalizations for bad behavior (instead of boundaries)

- Immediately trusting others (instead of letting trust develop appropriately based on trustworthy behavior)

- Thinking love conquers all or that feelings matter most (staying in a relationship based upon how they feel about the person instead of how they are being treated)

- Avoiding conflict or confrontation (not being assertive, "going with the flow," people-pleasing behavior)

- Being "go with the flow" (there is no solid sense of self; adjusting who they are based on what they feel others will approve of)

- Continual self-doubt (looking to others for validation or answers)

- Low degree of self-protection (an inability to determine when they are being mistreated, abused, in danger, or how to protect themselves when this happens).

While minimizing the above personality traits will help you

live a more empowered life in general, with all people, it is essential to realize that abuse is never the fault of the one being abused, whatever personality traits they may possess. Abusive behavior is the fault of the abuser. *To protect yourself, spend some time thinking about how you will and won't tolerate being treated in a relationship, how you will handle things if someone crosses your boundaries, and what you consider a deal-breaker.* Read that last sentence again, because truly understanding and embracing what that means will radically change your life.

Chapter 32: What types of questions should I ask when getting to know someone?

Dear Dana,

I've heard you say it's important to go slow and take time getting to know someone while dating—to think of dating like a job interview, screening the other person to see if they are a good fit. I thought I was doing this, but I keep dating men that turn out to be inconsiderate jerks. I realized that I'm not sure what type of questions I should be asking or traits to look for. Thoughts?

~ Beth

Dear Beth,

I used to encourage people to take things slow when dating someone, and then I added the "treat this process like a job interview" because I found that what people were initially hearing when I was saying, "go slow," was "don't have sex right away." While waiting to have sex is part of going slow, what needs to happen during this time is getting to know each other. The following are some questions to explore during this time. Keep in mind that there will be three different answers, one for you, one for him, and one for how you both really handle these topics within a relationship. The last part of how you "really" handle things is vital, as most of us tend to over-estimate how well we handle difficult situations. So this isn't a question that can be answered with words; it's a question that can only be answered with actions.

- Are each of you accountable for your actions?

- Is there sincere acknowledgment when feelings are hurt or boundaries crossed?

- How do each of you handle stress, frustration, and anger?

- How are successes and failures handled?

- Do either of you have expectations in terms of gender roles for men and women?

- How does he treat women, such as his mother, sister, or women that he has brief interactions with such a waitress?

Do you have respect for each other? Are there ways that either of you feel disrespected?

- Are the two of you able to negotiate, compromise, and work as a team?

- How does he feel about housework? How do you feel about housework?

- What are each of your thoughts on if you want to have children, along with how to raise and discipline them?

- How does each person handle money?

- What is the long-term plan in terms of each person's career?

- What is your social life like with him? Do you like his friends and family, and does he like yours? If there are problematic family members, are there boundaries and clear expectations with how much time is spent with them?

- Do you trust each other? Do you trust each other enough to combine bank accounts or go into business together?

- How is his credit? How is yours?

- Are there any double standards? For example, does he expect you to be on time, but he's always late? Or do you expect him to tell you who is with or what he's doing but you feel justified in being secretive?

- Do the two of you have a compatible sense of humor?

- Do you enjoy spending time together? Is he someone that you can talk to about your day or things on your mind, and vice-versa?

- What do you think he or you will be like in ten years? What do you think your life with him would be like in ten years? How about twenty? Is this the kind of life and partner that you would like?

- Are issues able to be resolved, or do conversations go in circles?

Many of these questions can be uncomfortable to ask or answer, and some are more significant than others. If you come across what you find to be deal-breaker behavior, remember that it's okay to stop seeing someone. You don't need to continue dating them because you feel you owe them a chance or don't want to be judgmental. The process of dating is all about discernment. If there is ever a time to go slow and be choosey about who and what you want in your life, this is it.

Chapter 33: How many red flags should I see before I consider it all a deal breaker?

Dear Dana,

I got out of an abusive relationship about five months ago, and have recently started dating again. The guy I've been dating is very different from my ex. He's kind, considerate, and makes me a top priority in his life; however, there are some red flags. I suppose the main one is that he still talks to many of his exes. My last boyfriend cheated on me non-stop, so I know I'm probably overly sensitive about this. When I asked him why he talks to his exes, he told me that they are just friends and that they mean nothing to him, but he also did say that he had a "friends with benefits" type relationship with two of them before we began dating seriously. I don't want to be jealous or controlling, and I know the whole "friends with benefits" thing seems to be fairly common with people these days. Am I wrong for having a problem with this? Is this a red flag, or am I overly sensitive? How many red flags are a problem?

~ Susan

Dear Susan,

I don't think you are overly sensitive about him still having regular communication with women that he has had sex with. It's one thing for a person to have platonic friends, but even that can be problematic in a relationship, as with platonic friendships, it's not uncommon for one person to have feelings for the other. However, if a person has been sexual with their "friends," then they aren't just friends. It's reasonable, and appropriate, to have an issue with your partner spending time with people they've dated. The more significant issue has to do with how he responds to your feelings about him spending time with these women. If he's willing to let his "friendships" with these women that "mean nothing" to him hurt or end his relationship with you, then this shows you that your relationship is worth less than nothing to him.

I also want to mention that it's essential for you to get grounded in what is and isn't acceptable behavior in terms of a partner, because you are right about the "friends with benefits" thing being common these days. And because of that, you will most likely get a wide variety of advice from other people regarding your thoughts about it. We could go back and forth forever, trying to figure out if you are making a big deal out of things, or if he is cheating, or if these women are only friends, but at the end of the day, it doesn't matter. It also doesn't matter how many red flags a person has. If a person has one major red flag, then that's enough. You don't need to wait for the red flags to reach a certain number before you walk away. What matters is if someone has actions you aren't okay with, and they defend those actions or aren't willing to sincerely change. If you aren't comfortable with him spending time with women he's had sex with, that's reasonable. It's okay for you to tighten up your deal-breakers to include any situation that causes mental anguish, perpetual confusion, unnecessary jealousy or insecurity, or any relationship that feels emotionally unsafe. The more you know yourself and what does and doesn't work for you, the easier it becomes to make decisions about whether to stay or go.

Chapter 34: How long does it take to be ready to date after abuse?

Dear Dana,

How long does it take most people to be ready to date again? I've been single for three years now, and I still have no sex drive or interest in dating. It's not that I'm scared to date; it's just that I feel numb and have no interest.

~ Brenda

Dear Brenda,

An abusive relationship is a traumatic relationship. And after any type of trauma—especially relationship trauma—it's common to feel numb, disconnected, and have a loss of interest in things that were once enjoyable. Sometimes this numbness is due to depression, PTSD, or shifting from "fight-or-flight" to a prolonged "freeze" mode. Everyone's timeframe and desire to date or be sexual is different. It's not uncommon for those who have experienced abuse to have no desire to date for several years, or if they do date, to feel numb or disinterested in dating or having sex. This lack of interest can cause a person to fear that they are forever broken and will never connect with others in a meaningful way.

Have you ever used a lawnmower that's sat in the garage for a while? If so, then you know you can't just pull the cord and expect it to start right up. First, you have to push the button on the side that releases a bit of fuel into the line before you attempt to start it. This is called priming the pump, and reconnecting with your sexuality can be very much the same way.

What helps is to change up your emotional and physical environment as well as your mindset. What I mean by this is: if you have physical reminders of your ex all over your home, try rearranging your furniture, or painting the walls a different color. You could also make a list of all the things your ex didn't want to do with you or wouldn't allow you to do, and then you could start doing them. It can be difficult to move forward if our environment is full of reminders of the past. If you haven't already changed up the energy in your home, you may be surprised as to how different you feel after making a handful of small shifts.

Changing your physical appearance helps send both conscious and subconscious signals to yourself and others that you have entered the next chapter in your life. In terms of reclaiming your sexuality, it helps to make it your own before you start dating again. So instead of relying on another person to make you feel attractive or sexual, reconnect with these feelings on your own. The added benefit is that the more you are familiar and comfortable with your body, the more enjoyable sex can be. The reason for this is so that you know what you like and don't like, because many women aren't familiar with their body and rely on their partner to satisfy them.

Reclaiming your sexuality goes a long way in boosting confidence, as it's no longer coming from an outside source. Some ways to do this are to invest in bras, panties, and pajamas that you feel cute or sexy in, and wear them regularly. Don't reserve them for a special date night. This way you start to get more in tune with your sexuality so that when you do decide to share it with someone, *they are getting to experience it—they aren't the cause of it.*

Additionally, I encourage you not to wait until you feel aroused or are in a romantic relationship to be sexual. Allowing yourself to take the time to explore your body while thinking about something erotic (or someone besides your ex) can help to reclaim your body and sexuality. Reaching an orgasm on your own allows you to feel good instead of relying on someone else to make you feel a certain way.

Once you begin giving yourself the time to feel attractive, and to feel pleasure your own way, your attitude towards your sexuality will start to shift. This doesn't mean that you will find yourself wanting to date but, at a minimum, you may find that you feel more comfortable in your skin.

Chapter 35: Is there a connection between narcissism and thoughtlessness?

Dear Dana,

My ex proposed with a cheap ring that wasn't at all my style. It felt like there was no effort put into it, and I'm trying to determine if there is a connection between narcissism and being thoughtless.

~ Molly

Dear Molly,

Every narcissist, abuser, or person in general, is different. Some are selfish, cheap, and put little to no thought into the gifts they give others—even engagement rings. However, others come across as selfless, lavish spenders, and thoughtful, planning out holidays and vacations (although, this is usually to make themselves look good, not because they care about the other person). These types of narcissistic abusers love the praise and adoration that comes from their target's friends and family who will then believe that; the narcissist is this wonderful person.

Because everyone is different, looking at the amount of money or thought someone puts into a gift isn't the best way to determine the level of respect or thoughtfulness a person may have. Granted, if someone gives a gift that is an afterthought, not personal, or the bare minimum then, yes, that tends to be an indicator of that person's level of emotional investment in the other person. However, odds are this is probably long-standing behavior on their end, and you've already experienced a lot of inconsiderate and selfish behavior from them.

A better way to tell if a person respects you is to see how they respond to your boundaries, and how they treat you when they are irritated, frustrated, or angry. It's easy to respect others when we feel like it, but when we are upset with them, that's when the truth comes out. It's reasonable to expect people to control their temper and be respectful even when they are upset and angry. After all, we expect this in other environments, such as at work or in public. For some reason, many people tend to think that it's okay to treat poorly those closest to them. This is a problem and sign of blurred or non-existent boundaries.

So, whether or not a narcissist appears thoughtful, the real question is: do you feel treated with respect? And if you don't, are you able to assert yourself?

Chapter 36: Do I need to wait until I'm healed before I date again?

Dear Dana,

People keep telling me that I need to wait until I'm fully healed before I start dating. I'm not sure what they mean by this or what that would even look like. It's been about six months since my ex left me, and while I'm still hurt by how he treated me, I no longer feel emotionally blown apart, and I'm not crying every day like I used to. I guess I think that I'm doing pretty well these days considering what I went through. Do I need to wait until I'm completely healed before I date again, and if so, how will I know when I'm there?

~ Sophia

Dear Sophia,

I, too, used to encourage people to wait until they've healed before they start dating; however, I've since realized two important things: 1. What people think healing is, and what healing *really* is are two very different things, 2. Many of our wounds stay hidden and only become activated once we are in a romantic relationship. So, for that reason, there is only so much healing we can do when we are single.

The word "healing" can be vague, and it means more than feeling emotionally balanced most of the time—although this is a wonderful and important step. So let's take a look at what healing is and isn't.

Some common misconceptions about healing are:

- That you will return to who you used to be.

- That you will trust people as you did before.

- That being in an abusive relationship couldn't happen again because you know the red flags to watch out for.

- That being in an abusive relationship won't happen again because a person is only allowed so much hurt in this lifetime, or because the last relationship was bad luck, like getting hit by lightning, and lightning doesn't strike the same place twice.

- That any issues you have with your new partner are due to the abusive dynamic you had with your previous partner.

- That, if you no longer feel emotionally devastated, fixated on your ex, or suicidal, that you are healed and ready to date.

- That healing is a straight line.

What healing really means:

- Knowing when you are being mistreated and how to respond appropriately when this happens.

- Knowing when you are being treated in a way that is uncomfortable, or that isn't okay with you, and being able to validate yourself that what you are experiencing is a problem.

- Knowing how to assert your wants, needs, and boundaries.

- Knowing what your deal breakers are and implementing them when necessary.

- Being able to set the pace, and moving at a reasonable pace.

- Being able to express your emotions appropriately.

- Not looking for a relationship, or another person to, make you feel loved, safe, happy, fulfilled, or okay with life.

- Understanding what makes behavior dysfunctional or functional.

- Understanding your own dysfunctional and functional thoughts and actions.

- Being able to form your own opinions and to take action on them.

- Being able to identify how we feel about others' behavior and how to respond to it in a tactful, mature way.

- Cultivating an honest, healthy relationship with yourself. In large part, this means acknowledging and accepting your thoughts, feelings, likes, and dislike.

This list of what healing really means probably feels overwhelming. Please know that becoming a healthy, well-adjusted adult who handles everything appropriately is more of a journey than a destination. Whenever we learn a new skill (let alone a series of new skills), we experience a learning curve that can feel discouraging at times. Learning to walk comes with a lot of stumbling and falling, and so does learning to set boundaries and cultivating a healthy relationship with ourselves. Stumbling and falling are part of learning, and it's vital to give yourself compassion and grace along the way. However, with that said, I think there is a base level of healing that needs to be in place before a person is ready to date again. If I had to pare down the list above, I'd say that it's essential for a person to:

1. Know when you are being treated in a way that makes you uncomfortable, and then being tactfully assertive about this. It helps to understand the connection between what's going on in your life and how you feel. For example, if you feel irritated, upset, offended, etc. because these are all signs that someone has crossed one of your boundaries. And then it is important not to be swayed by others who may think you are over-sensitive, exaggerating, and so forth.

2. Turn to a therapist, social worker, life coach or spiritual advisor if you feel the need to talk through and process the abuse. While sharing the traumatic experiences in our life with loved ones can create closeness, if we are over-relying on friends or our new partners to heal us this will create an imbalance in our relationships. This imbalance leads to us being dependent, and puts them in a place of possibly feeling overwhelmed, pressured, and resentful.

3. Learn about assertive communication, boundaries, standards, and deal-breakers, and practice them with everyone, not just those you date.

4. Know that trusting others is something which takes time, and that deep levels of trust aren't to be freely given. For deep levels of trust to be given, emotional safety must be present. And for emotional safety to be present, enough time has the be spent with a person to see how they handle stress, fear, anger, frustration, in addition to the more significant or vulnerable things you share with them. If they handle these things appropriately, and don't use them against you, tease you about them, or invalidate you, then these are early signs that a degree of emotional safety is developing. [The basics of these skills are best practiced in a low-risk environment, such as with acquaintances rather than with family or friends. The reason for this is that it's much easier to practice setting boundaries, asserting yourself, and seeing the behavior of others clearly if there isn't a deep emotional investment in them. If we start practicing these skills with family and friends first, it's a lot like learning how to swim by jumping into the deep end of the pool. If you are looking to expand your social circle to practice these skills or just have some fun, consider visiting the website meetup.com. This site allows you to connect with others based on shared interests and

hobbies. Once you have practiced your new skills in a low-risk environment, then consider moving on to dating.

If you are with a person who has shown themselves to be emotionally safe, who has assertive communication, and who is open to discussing your fears and feelings, then it can help to share your feelings about healing with them. Doing so isn't the same as making them responsible for your feelings. They can't fix you, and even if they could, that's too much to put on another person and will lead to burnout on their end.

A healthy way to communicate your fears to your partner is to let them know, for example, if they are upset with you, for them to preface any confrontation by saying something like, "I love you, and I'm not going anywhere. I was hurt yesterday when you did xyz." Or letting them know that if they get upset and go silent or create an icy chill in the air, that this makes you anxious (this kind of behavior makes almost everyone anxious), and that if they are upset could they tell you and then let you know a time frame for when they will be ready to discuss what is bothering them. If you do this, it's important to communicate what you need from them as well as to understand that they may or may not be willing or able to communicate with you in such an open way. If this is the case, then you will have to re-evaluate the relationship and see what level of communication you need with a partner.

Like I mentioned before, there is only so much healing we can do outside of a romantic relationship. Once you do begin dating, you may find yourself struggling with feelings of anxiety, fearing that perhaps this new person is too good to be true; or you may see quite a few red flags and wonder if you're making a big deal out of nothing. You may also feel chronic anxiety, holding your breath, waiting for another side of them to surface. Or perhaps you fear that they might up and leave you at any time. Though challenging, these feelings are all normal and do not necessarily mean you are not healed enough to date. But do study the list of what healing really means and consider where you might still have some work to do. Also, be aware that things will come up in the context of dating that was not possible to anticipate ahead of time. Being healed doesn't mean these things won't happen, but instead that you have the tools to address them.

Any of us can have triggers and not know it until they are activated, and there's a good chance this will happen once you begin dating again. This reactivation of triggers does not mean that you aren't ready to date. For example, let's say the person you are dating says something about wanting to get a birthday card for his mother, and instantly you feel upset, not realizing that you've been triggered because your abusive-ex had always triangulated you and his mother. An experience like that could not have been anticipated and doesn't mean that you aren't ready to date again. The big takeaway here is that we need to learn how to recognize when we are triggered and how to handle it appropriately.

Here's an example of a boundary being crossed that would only happen if you were dating. Let's say that your new partner enjoys holding your hand and giving you small kisses in public, and maybe you aren't comfortable with this. On the surface, this level of public affection isn't necessarily a sign that your partner is a problematic person; it's that they show more public affection than you are comfortable with. If you've never dated someone who was affectionate in public, then you might find yourself struggling with how to speak up and set limits with your new partner. Now, if after you voice your concerns they continue their behavior as though what you said didn't matter, then this is a problem as they aren't respecting your boundaries. If this is the case, then it might be time to re-evaluate the relationship.

Conclusion

It's been my experience that people tend to read a book like this in one of two ways. If they are new to this topic, they most likely see each question, and answer, as separate. However, if they are deeply familiar with this topic, they may see patterns between the questions and even more similarities between the answers.

An abusive relationship is a complicated relationship, and the confusion doesn't end when the relationship ends. It takes time to sort through the various disempowering and dysfunctional messages that go along with abuse, and the beginning stages involve seeing each question and answer as unrelated. This is normal, not only for abuse but for learning anything new. It takes some time to see how concepts are related, whether that be with understanding emotional health or learning to play the piano. For the sake of clarity, here are what I believe to be the six main takeaways from the responses given in this book.

6 Main takeaways:

1. You don't need to get clarity as to whether someone else's problematic behavior is a sign of a personality disorder or if they have bad intentions—all you need to know is that it's a problem for you. Think about spotting problematic/abusive behavior from a bottom-up, rather than top-down, kind of way. A top-down approach means to look at someone's behavior in a rigid and absolute way, such as something they are doing is either a sign they are personality disordered, abusive, cheating, or not. When we think we should be able to see all problematic behavior right away, we are setting ourselves up for frustration. However, if we take a bottom-up approach, we shift the focus off of trying to psychoanalyze their behavior or guess their intentions to tuning in to how we feel about their behavior, and then acting accordingly. Understanding behavior in a bottom-up kind of way is the ONLY way to make your life work because it is about being in tune with knowing when we are uncomfortable or had a boundary crossed. If we are taking a top-down approach, we often second guess ourselves and turn to others for validation and advice. When we take a bottom-up approach, we can validate ourselves and don't need others to agree with our choices.

2. There is no such thing as being too sensitive. If someone says or does something that upsets you, it's not because you are too sensitive, it's because they crossed a line with you. Everyone has soft spots; it's part of being human. Additionally, what each person finds funny or appropriate is different. For example, if you become upset or hurt when someone teases you about the way you look or act, this doesn't mean that you are too sensitive but that this is a sensitive area for you and you don't like people interacting with you in that way. If you tell them that you don't find teasing or jokes aimed at you funny, and they dismiss your concerns and/or continue making jabs, they aren't respecting your boundaries. Their lack of regard doesn't mean that you are too sensitive; it means that they are insensitive.

3. You can tell when your boundaries are crossed based on how you feel. Everyone's boundaries are different, and no one knows where yours are until you make them known. While this is true, you also don't need to educate somebody on the basics of respectful, adult behavior. If you are dating someone who, for example, yells, curses, hits, shoves, or threatens, you would be wasting your time telling them that their behavior is not okay because it is obviously outside the bounds of mature adult behavior. If an adult doesn't know that behaving this way isn't okay, they have much larger issues. Also, a person's boundaries are continually shifting based on various features such as mood, maturity, self-awareness, the situation, people involved, and context. For example, how your friend jokes with you might be fine, but if your boss or a stranger were to joke with you in the same way, you might not be okay with that. This is common as we all have people in different circles and interact with them accordingly.

You can tell when your boundaries are crossed based on how you feel. Confusion, irritation, anger, or resentment are all common feelings we experience when someone has crossed a line with us. When our boundaries are functional, we don't rehash conversations, or feel anxious and uncomfortable around someone. We feel comfortable, like taking a bath in water that is the right temperature. We aren't thinking about the temperature; we are just enjoying the experience.

4. Love without boundaries or deal-breakers isn't love; it's a recipe for resentment, frustration, anxiety, and abuse. It's important to know where you begin and end and where others begin and end. When boundaries are blurred, the results leads to a wide range of dysfunctional relationships, such as: parents treating minor children like friends, or adults treating other adults like children, adults trying to control others, or adults seeking others (sometimes their own children) to take charge and take care of them. To have a healthy relationship, you must have healthy boundaries, know when they are crossed, and how to handle this when it happens.

5. Having deal-breakers is part of having healthy boundaries. While knowing where your boundaries are is essential, it's also vital to understand where your deal breakers are and when it's time to walk away. Continually asserting yourself with those who cross your boundaries is a sign of weak boundaries. For example, if a person is in a relationship with someone who repeatedly flirts with other people, no matter how much they are told this isn't okay, then the relationship is just spinning in a circle. The other person knows what they are doing isn't okay, as you've said it before. If they keep doing it, then it's time for you to do something other than reminding them of what they already know. This is where deal breakers come into play. Additionally, healthy deal-breakers involve more than being cheated on or physically harmed. If these are a person's only two deal-breakers, this doesn't make them dedicated to their relationship, or compassionate; it means they are willing to be mistreated in a multitude of other ways to keep this relationship going. (And it would be worthwhile for the person to examine the reasons they are willing to be mistreated.)

6. Healthy relationships are created—not found. For a healthy relationship to develop, both people need to know where their boundaries are, when they are crossed, and how to be assertive when that happens. Also, healthy relationships only have the chance to develop when each person can be emotionally supportive and available. A healthy relationship cannot be created through one person's efforts alone, or with one healthy person trying to change the other. This unequal dynamic is at the core of most codependent relationships and is worth examining if you've found yourself in this "helper" or "fixer" role time and again.

The foundation of a healthy relationship is two people who have the basics of healthy communication, accountability for their behavior, and the ability to be mature during times of stress and disagreement. It is created when emotional safety is present, which means you trust the other person enough to be vulnerable with them, you feel safe disagreeing. Trust is built through time and action. Does this person's behavior allow for you to be vulnerable and open with them? Are you able to negotiate, speak up, have your feelings honored? There is no such thing as a person with whom you will never have a conflict, or who will always know exactly where your boundaries are, but a healthy relationship is created when both partners address these problems, as they arise, in a respectful, solutions-oriented manner

And perhaps most importantly of all...

Please know that as you begin to reconnect with your authentic thoughts, feelings, wants, and needs, your life will begin to come into focus at a level that you may have never experienced before. This process is a gradual unfolding, or blooming, and occurs moment-by-moment. As this takes place, you will have a much clearer understanding of your boundaries, standards, and deal-breakers within a wide range of settings. While such massive changes may seem like an overwhelming amount of work, please know that this process is about unbecoming everything you aren't so you can be who you have always been. I wish you all the best in this next chapter of your life, and I hope it's the best one yet.

~ *Dana*

About the Author

Dana Morningstar is an abuse educator, focusing on awareness and prevention, as well as recovery, healing, and self-esteem. She seeks to empower those who have been abused to reclaim their power, boundaries, confidence, and identity. In addition to being an author, she has a blog, podcast, runs a large support group, and hosts a three-hour live stream every Wednesday night on her YouTube channel, "Thrive After Abuse." In her free time, she enjoys relaxing on Lake Michigan, practicing aerial yoga, reading, and gardening.

CPSIA information can be obtained
at www.ICGtesting.com
Printed in the USA
LVHW041016210820
663704LV00004B/268